GAME | A STEP-BY-STEP
FISHING | HANDBOOK

GAME FISHING

A STEP-BY-STEP HANDBOOK

Expert advice on game fish, casting techniques, flies and fly tying, with over 280 practical photographs and diagrams to show skills and equipment

Peter Gathercole
Consultant Editor: Bruce Vaughan

southwater

This edition is published by Southwater, an imprint of Anness Publishing Ltd, Hermes House, 88–89 Blackfriars Road, London SE1 8HA; tel. 020 7401 2077; fax 020 7633 9499

www.southwaterbooks.com; www.annesspublishing.com

If you like the images in this book and would like to investigate using them for publishing, promotions or advertising, please visit our website www.practicalpictures.com for more information.

UK agent: The Manning Partnership Ltd; tel. 01225 478444; fax 01225 478440; sales@manning-partnership.co.uk

UK distributor: Grantham Book Services Ltd; tel. 01476 541080; fax 01476 541061; orders@gbs.tbs-ltd.co.uk

North American agent/distributor: National Book Network; tel. 301 459 3366; fax 301 429 5746; www.nbnbooks.com

Australian agent/distributor: Pan Macmillan Australia; tel. 1300 135 113; fax 1300 135 103; customer.service@macmillan.com.au

New Zealand agent/distributor: David Bateman Ltd; tel. (09) 415 7664; fax (09) 415 8892

Publisher: Joanna Lorenz
Senior Editor: Doreen Palamartschuk
Editor: Anthony Atha
Designer: James Lawrence
Special photography: Sue Ford and Peter Gathercole
Illustrators: Mike Atkinson (species),
Dave Batten (rigs and diagrams)
Editorial Reader: Kate Henderson
Indexer: Hilary Bird
Production Controller: Yolande Denny

ETHICAL TRADING POLICY

Because of our ongoing ecological investment programme, you, as our customer, can have the pleasure and reassurance of knowing that a tree is being cultivated on your behalf to naturally replace the materials used to make the book you are holding. For further information about this scheme, go to www.annesspublishing.com/trees

A CIP catalogue record for this book is available from the British Library.

Previously published as part of *The Practical Guide to Game Fishing*

Contents

Game Fishing

In fishing parlance, game fishing means fishing for members of the salmonidae family: salmon, sea trout, brown trout, rainbow trout and grayling, and it is difficult to say precisely why these fish have such a fascination for anglers. Other fish, notably the big sea fish such as sharks and tope, fight harder. Some coarse fish are more difficult to outwit and capture, and a number of coarse fish such as carp and barbel, are renowned for their strength and guile when they have been hooked.

It is true that game fish, particularly salmon and sea trout, make a notable contribution to the table, but many would prefer to eat Dover sole or fresh turbot, and some trout caught in reservoirs can taste rather indifferent. Nevertheless, game fishing retains its hold on many anglers and can provide the pinnacle of an angler's career.

Introduction

The reason for the fascination of game fishing is probably a combination of factors. First of all there is the challenge of outwitting the quarry: shy trout in chalk streams are easily scared and can be infuriatingly choosy when they are feeding on one particular natural fly. If the angler is to be successful, he or she must identify and imitate that fly to stand any chance of success. The capture of a large chalk-stream trout is something to be celebrated.

ABOVE: The capture of a fresh-run salmon on a fly has been described as "one of the great moment's in the joy of life".

The Right Conditions

Trout in lakes and reservoirs can feed on many different creatures at many different depths in the water, and the angler has to solve a number of problems successfully. Salmon and sea trout will only take freely when conditions are favourable, which they seldom are, and even then they may not take when conditions seem absolutely right. Salmon, sea trout and many rainbows also fight with great strength and determination and all game fish can be extremely choosy about the type of baits or flies they will accept.

Probably the main reason why game fishing holds such a fascination is the rivers, lakes and lochs where it takes place. Salmon rivers and Highland lochs, particularly, are

BELOW: The River Test at Kimbridge, Hampshire. The Test is the most famous of all the chalk streams of southern England and can provide a great challenge for the angler.

places of supreme beauty and the fisherman is conscious of being surrounded by and being close to nature. The primitive hunting instinct that exists in all anglers thrives in beautiful locations. The game fish described in this book are five in number although many anglers place the grayling as a coarse fish for it breeds in the spring and has the same season as coarse fish. However both the grayling and brown trout are to be found in unpolluted clear streams and the grayling is particularly sensitive to the quality of the water.

Brown trout are found all over the country in both rivers and stillwaters and nowadays are frequently stocked in reservoirs and lakes. The finest trout fishing is on the chalk streams of southern England, where the water is crystal clear, and the fishing exacting in the extreme. Trout fishing, generally, is a local pursuit and many anglers fish for trout near where they live, although with the advent of

stocked waters populated by enormous fish, bred for their size, more and more anglers are visiting far waters in search of these monsters.

Rainbow trout, too, have become very popular for they generally fight better than brown trout and they are easy to stock in all waters, not just reservoirs and lakes, for they tolerate higher water temperatures and poorer water quality than the native brown trout. They grow quicker and commercially offer a better return.

Species Under Threat

The game fish that have had to struggle to survive are the two migratory species where humankind is unable to give a helping hand and the environment changes have worked against them. Sea trout in particular have suffered, firstly from UDN (ulcerative dermal necrosis) disease in the 1960s that virtually wiped out the population on many rivers, and latterly with offshore pollution caused by the salmon farms in the estuaries, particularly around the west coast of Scotland. Sea trout have also suffered because the sandeel, their main diet in the sea, has been badly overfished by commercial fishermen for use as fertilizer and to make fish pellets. Some rivers in Wales still support a good number of sea trout but in many places their survival is in doubt.

The plight of the salmon is well-documented and many rivers are now taking drastic steps to preserve their stock by banning all methods of fishing except the fly and insisting on fish being returned to the river unharmed so that they have a chance

of spawning and reproducing the species. These matters are the concern of every angler and it is important to all that the salmon and sea trout continue to run and spawn in the 21st century.

It is the capture of these species that is the summit of the angler's ambition. There is no doubt that the hooking, playing and landing of a salmon is one of the great moments in an angler's life. Sea trout, too, hooked in the dark on a river when they take with a great jolt on the line, or coming to the dap on a Highland loch with a heart-stopping splash are a quarry fit for all.

BELOW: Fishing the sedge rise as the sun sets on Rutland Water.

Tackle

Modern tackle has made game fishing a great deal easier. Rods are lighter and more powerful: modern technology has led to the development of many different types of line that make casting easier; and various lines can be purchased that will sink through the water at different rates or float on the surface. Nylon leaders are stronger and thinner and modern nylon can be virtually invisible in water. Flies and lures also are now made from modern materials that are better than many old-fashioned ones and the design of salmon flies, in particular, has improved drastically.

BOTTOM LEFT: A variety of duns and spinners in a dry-fly fisher's fly box.

ABOVE LEFT: Fishing the evening rise on the River Wharfe, Yorkshire, in a fall of spinners.

ABOVE: Netting a good rainbow trout in spring on a north of England reservoir.

Also game fishing is now available to everyone. Whereas years ago most of the best game fishing was in private hands and reserved, nowadays much of the best trout fishing is on modern reservoirs where anyone can buy a day ticket, and even if the best salmon beats are still prohibitively expensive there are tickets available on a number of local waters in Scotland with the chance of a fish.

BELOW: Changing the fly on a successful day fishing a loch in the Orkneys.

Species

Atlantic Salmon *(Salmo salar)*

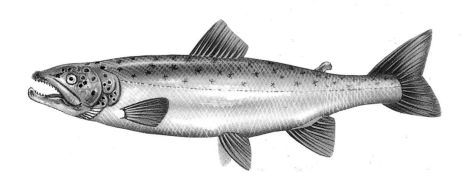

Recognition

For many freshwater game anglers the Atlantic salmon, *Salmo salar*, is the greatest prize of all. Fresh in from the tide it is a magnificent fish. Bright silver flanks, occasionally flushed with a tinge of purple, are contrasted by a dark steely back. The body is muscular and streamlined, the tail pointed. Often the fish has sea lice still attached and, as these soon fall off once the fish has left the sea, they are a good indication as to how fresh it is. Its perfection slowly diminishes the longer the salmon remains in freshwater. Silver flanks dull and become coloured, the fish lose condition, and the males develop reddish brown spots, red diagonal squares and a large hooked jaw, known as a kype. Fish like this are coming into spawning condition and if caught should always be returned. Although salmon spawn during October to December, they enter the river at any month of the year so one may have spent a full year in freshwater, living off its accumulated fat.

Habitat and Location

Atlantic salmon occur from the east coast of the United States and Canada, across northern Europe and Scandinavia and into Russia. They are also found as far south as northern Spain and Portugal. In the UK they are found throughout the river systems of Scotland, Wales, northern England, the West Country and the west coast of Ireland.

Behaviour and Feeding Habits

Salmon are anadromous, living and feeding at sea but returning to freshwater to reproduce. Once a male and female salmon have paired off, a depression or redd is cut in the gravel, the female lays her eggs and the male fertilizes them with his milt. The fertilized eggs take approximately a hundred days to hatch after which the tiny alevins stay buried in the gravel for several weeks. Once the yolk sac has been absorbed the baby salmon, now called fry, leave the redd and begin to feed. As the fry grow they develop into parr and then eventually into silver-flanked smolts, a process which can take from two to four years. The young salmon are now ready to migrate downstream to the sea, which they do in May.

After leaving the river of their birth most salmon feed in the ocean around Greenland and the Faroe Islands, returning to spawn one, two or three years later. Salmon that spend only one winter at sea are known as grilse, and return to their rivers during mid summer. They weigh from 4–8 lb (1.81–3.63 kg).

LEFT: **Fly fishing for salmon in summer. The Castle Connel water, River Shannon. In the summer most anglers fish with floating lines and small flies.**

ABOVE: A spring salmon caught fishing from a boat in the lower beat of the River Beauly.

The fish that return to their rivers after more than one winter at sea normally weigh from 6–20 lb (2.72–9.07 kg). Atlantic salmon can reach 70 lb (32 kg) or more, but fish this size are extremely rare and very few fish over 30 lb (13.6 kg) are caught by anglers.

Salmon can be caught in both rivers and lakes. They are reliant on rain to trigger their migration into the river, and in smaller rivers in summer when the water is low, large numbers build up in the estuary. When the rain comes and the river rises and colours they pour upstream, resting every now and then behind rocks – in fact

anywhere that provides protection from the powerful current. This urge to run is very strong, and salmon leap falls and other major obstructions such as weirs on their way to reach their spawning grounds.

In the UK salmon rivers fall into two main types. The larger east coast Scottish rivers, the Tweed, Spey and Tay, do require reasonable amounts of water for the salmon to run, but even in normal summer conditions fish will continue to enter them in limited numbers. The smaller spate rivers on the other hand are more dependent on rain for them to contain salmon. Many are fast flowing and rocky; the rain soon runs off, and the peak times to fish can be only a few hours after the river level starts to fall, let alone days. As salmon do not feed in freshwater the angler has to try and stimulate the old feeding response in the fish, and good water conditions are very important for this.

Spring and autumn are the best times of the year to catch a larger fish and each year some salmon over 30 lb (13.6 kg) are caught both on fly and spinner. Unfortunately these runs of big fish, especially the "springers", have become increasingly rare, largely because of netting on the high seas,

and on many rivers anglers now return these fish in an effort to maintain stocks. Fish are also held in hatcheries and stripped at spawning time and the fry returned to the rivers to increase the stock.

Apart from when the river is in flood, salmon can be caught on the fly right through the season, although techniques need to be altered to suit the conditions. When the river is still high and cold during spring, fishing a deep sunk line and a large fly is the most effective tactic. On smaller rivers and even on larger ones when the water is low it is quite possible to catch salmon on trout tackle. Indeed during very low water conditions a size 10 or 12 fly fished on a 7 weight rod can actually be more effective than standard salmon tackle.

Salmon can also be caught in lochs, particularly in Scotland and Ireland. The usual method is to troll from a boat around rocky headlands and other well-known holding areas. When fly fishing the boat is allowed to drift side-on to the wind in classic loch style. A floating line and a team of three wet flies are used – patterns such as the Black Pennell, Peter Ross and Kate MacLaren are effective. Due to the size and power of the fish, leader strength should be 8–10 lb (3.63–4.54 kg).

Occasionally there is some confusion as to whether the fish caught is a salmon or sea trout, especially when it is fresh and bright silver. There are a few pointers to help identification. For example in salmon the tail is forked and the wrist at the tail base wide enough to be gripped easily, whereas in the sea trout the tail is square or convex and the wrist too thin to be gripped securely. Also when the mouth is closed the rear edge of the salmon's upper lip is level with the rear of its eye while in the sea trout it reaches beyond it. Additionally the salmon's spots are X-shaped rather than round as in the sea trout.

LEFT: Spinning for salmon in early spring on the Dalguise water, River Tay. Fish enter the Tay system from December the previous year, and fishing on Loch Tay traditionally starts the season on 1st January each year.

RIGHT: A fresh-run summer salmon in the peak of condition caught on the fly. Most rivers have a run of smaller summer fish.

Sea Trout *(Salmo trutta)*

Recognition

Sea trout are the sea-run form of the brown trout and, like salmon, are anadromous, running from the sea to freshwater to spawn, although unlike salmon, sea trout will feed spasmodically when in fresh water. When they first enter the river, adult sea trout are bright silver with hardly any spots, but the longer they are in freshwater the darker they become, and towards the end of the season many are almost black. When they reach this stage they are nearly ready to spawn and if caught should be returned carefully.

Habitat and Location

Sea trout are found in much of the coastal water surrounding Ireland and the UK, along with much of northern Europe and Scandinavia. Like salmon they have been under a great deal of pressure in recent years, and in some

areas, most notably the west coast of Ireland, populations appear to have collapsed and many fisheries are experiencing very limited runs. Much of the blame has been placed on salmon farms, where great net cages containing thousands of salmon have sprung up in many coastal regions – just the areas where the sea trout live. What has caused the problem is not the salmon themselves but the sea lice which parasitize them. Although the farmers treat the salmon to kill this pest, the vast numbers of fish make easy hosts and mean that sea lice numbers have rocketed, infesting the wild sea trout which rapidly lose condition and die. Inshore and estuary netting also take their toll, considerably reducing the numbers of fish able to return to spawn, while the commercial fishing of sandeels to create the pellets for feeding the farmed salmon also reduces the sea trout's food supply.

However, it is not all bad news. Many waters such as those in Wales and the West Country, where salmon farming is not such an issue, still have good runs of sea trout including some very large fish well into double figures. Welsh rivers in particular, including the Dovey, Towy and Rheidol, have produced some wonderful sea trout fishing over the last few years.

Behaviour and Feeding Habits

When the sea trout comes into spawning condition it is far less reliant than the salmon on a large spate to induce it to run. While extra water will bring sea trout in to the

LEFT: Landing a good sea trout at night. Night fishing can be most exciting if the fish are taking well.

ABOVE: A fine sea trout caught at night in Wales. Note the square tail.

river system, they are quite capable of working their way upstream even in low summer levels. Although in exceptional circumstances sea trout will enter a river as early as March and as late as October, the main runs take place during the summer months from June through to September, with July and August being the peak months. Actual spawning takes place from October through to January. Like the salmon the sea trout goes through stages from egg through to parr and eventually smolt before heading for the sea.

Sea trout can be caught both in freshwater and saltwater. Traditionally they have been taken from lakes and rivers, but increasing numbers of anglers are finding areas where they can be caught from the sea shore. The west of Ireland, Scotland and Wales are the most productive coastlines, along with island groups such as the Orkneys and Shetlands. Tackle is quite

simple, either light spinning gear or medium-weight fly tackle similar to that used for reservoir lure fishing. Fly patterns are also similar, the most effective being large streamer patterns that imitate small fish.

While catching sea trout from saltwater is growing in popularity the majority of fish are still taken when they return to freshwater. In rivers they may be caught on bait, spinner or fly. Worm fishing is very effective, particularly when the water is high and coloured, while spinning with a small Mepps spinner or a light Quill Minnow is deadly when the river is clearing. The Quill Minnow can be particularly effective even in low water – and is often fished upstream rather than down.

When the river is low, typically at summer level, fly fishing comes into its own. Although sea trout can be caught on the fly during daylight if the water is still carrying a little colour, clear low water, under the cover of darkness is when they take best. Night fishing for sea trout is an exciting experience although not without its problems. Casting and

wading are the most obvious two and, if you are fishing a river for the first time, it is essential to observe the pools first in daylight to learn their characteristics before night falls.

When it is dark the shoals of sea trout, which during the day remain concealed under banks and in the deeper pools, move into the shallower water and are keen to take a fly. When the river is low small trout patterns such as the Butcher or the Peter Ross tied on a size 10 hook work well, but for normal conditions a larger fly such as the Blackie or the Medicine Fly is more effective. These may be fished on either a floating or slow-sinking line working the fly across and downstream.

On lakes and lochs sea trout may be caught on standard wet-fly tackle almost identical to that used for loch-style trout fishing. They are also caught dapping, where a large bushy fly is allowed to blow out in front of the boat on a floss line and bounced on the top of the water. They may also be caught on spinners, either cast and retrieved or trolled from a boat under power.

ABOVE: Fishing for sea trout on South Uist, Outer Hebrides, with a wet fly.

BELOW: A 3½ lb (1.59 kg) sea trout caught on a wet fly on Loch Hope in the far north of Scotland.

Brown Trout *(Salmo trutta)*

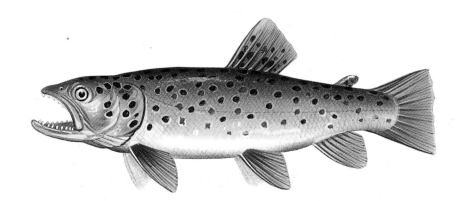

Current Records
British **25 lb 5 oz 12 drm (11.502 kg)**
World **40 lb 4oz (18.25 kg)**

Season
April to September. This can be longer in local reservoirs.

Distribution
Widespread in fast-running rivers and many stillwaters.

Natural Diet
Mayflies, caddisflies, stoneflies, midges, shrimps and small fish.

Top Spots
Chalk streams in southern England; reservoirs such as Grafham and Rutland Water.

Top Tip
Watch the water carefully and try to discover the fly the trout are feeding on.

Recognition

Brown trout are the indigenous species of trout throughout Britain and large parts of northern Europe. They grow large, well in excess of 20 lb (9.01 kg), but the average is nearer the 1 lb (0.45 kg) mark. They are extremely variable in colouration, which is largely dictated by the individual fish's habitat. Where the water is dark or peat-stained the fish themselves are often very dark with many large black spots. Conversely, where the trout are living over a light sandy bottom they are much lighter with either pale or silver flanks and much smaller and less profuse spots.

Most brown trout have a brownish-coloured back and pale, liberally spotted flanks. Normally there are no spots on the tail, which is a useful guide to distinguishing them from rainbow trout. Usually these flank spots are large and black, but occasionally, in trout living in small brooks, they can be mixed with a few red ones. Some populations also have bright-yellow bellies, giving them an extremely colourful appearance, yet in others the spots are almost absent, the flanks being bright silver and making the trout look very similar to its sea-run form, the sea trout.

Habitat and Location

Brown trout can be caught on a wide range of methods including bait, spinner and fly although in the UK, due mainly to fishery rules, most are taken on the latter. Although the brown trout is the natural species in the UK and Europe, fishing pressure and fluctuating water conditions mean that many are actually stocked in the same way as rainbow trout. However, due to the fact that the brown trout is less tolerant of high water temperatures and is slower growing than the rainbow, it is more expensive to produce and, as a result, stocked far less extensively. However, this still means that brown trout can be caught in many waters that would not normally contain them, most noticeably small put-and-take fisheries and large lowland reservoirs.

Some of the smaller waters, most famously Dever Springs in Hampshire and Felindre in South Wales, stock farmed brown trout of unnaturally huge proportions. Here fish of 10 lb (4.54 kg) or more are caught regularly and the cultivated record now stands at over 26 lb (11.8 kg). On reservoirs

LEFT: **Netting a wild trout on the River Wharfe in Yorkshire.**

TOP: **Returning a trout caught on the River Itchen, one of the famous chalk streams of southern England.**

ABOVE: **Three fine brown trout caught on a wet fly in Ireland.**

where the brown trout is stocked but must attain the bulk of its weight in the reservoir, a specimen brown trout would be classed as anything over 5 lb (2.27 kg). Even here there are very big grown-on fish, and each year venues such as Rutland Water and Grafham Water produce brown trout into double figures. In a river a trout over 4 lb (1.81 kg) is a prize specimen.

Most small lakes and reservoirs have to be stocked, but even some rivers which already contain indigenous populations of brown trout have their numbers supplemented with stock fish. While this makes the fishing initially better, it does raise the issue, should stock and wild fish interbreed, leading to the destruction of the wild fish's genetic integrity? To counteract this trend some enlightened fishery owners are now looking to habitat conservation and catch-and-release fishing to maintain viable, natural populations.

Almost all trout are caught on a fly, although spinning with minnows and fishing with a worm in small burns in Scotland and Wales is a good method for the young. The most sophisticated fishing is with a dry fly or nymph in a clear chalk stream, although wet flies are the normal method in stillwaters.

Brown trout in lakes provide the best wild brown trout fishing in the UK and Ireland. Because they are so large and less susceptible to over-fishing and loss of water through abstraction, many of our big natural lakes, particularly those in Scotland, northern England, Wales and the west coast of Ireland still contain substantial populations of brown trout. These fisheries have a long tradition of trout fishing, and the usual technique is loch style, casting a team of wet flies from a boat drifting side-on to the wind.

Dapping, too, where a large bushy fly or a natural insect, such as a daddy-longlegs (crane fly), is allowed to blow out in front of the boat, is also very effective. With dapping, instead of casting, a light floss line and a long rod, in excess of 12 ft (3.66 m), is used so that the breeze takes the fly out on to the water. While it catches all sizes of fish, the method has the reputation of tempting the larger specimens, and each year trout in excess of 10 lb (4.54 kg) are taken "on the dap".

Each year the largest natural brown trout are invariably caught by trolling a large spinner or dead-bait in one of the big Scottish lochs or Irish loughs that are known to hold these large fish. These ferox, as they are known, are highly predatory, forsaking a diet of small invertebrates

for fish such as perch and, especially, char which inhabit the deep water in these otherwise nutrient-poor lakes. This diet allows the ferox to attain weights of 10–15 lb (4.54–6.8 kg) with specimens up to 20 lb (9.07 kg) occasionally taken on rod and line.

Behaviour and Feeding Habits

Brown trout are highly territorial, particularly in rivers. Once a fish has established a feeding position it will defend it jealously, driving off other trout that come too close. Here the trout is in an ideal position to pick off the adults and nymphs of aquatic insects such as upwings, stoneflies and caddisflies, along with small crustaceans, as they drift downstream

ABOVE: **A good trout being brought to the net on Tal-y-Llyn in North Wales.**

with the current. Even on rivers brown trout have a taste for small fish and are not averse to taking bullheads and minnows, particularly early in the year when other forms of food are scarce.

Brown trout are found anywhere from tiny mountain streams to larger rain-fed rivers and rich, chalk streams. The size that the trout ultimately reach depends greatly on the available food supply and chalk-stream, loch and lough trout, with a plentiful diet of aquatic insects and crustaceans, are generally bigger than those found on rain-fed rivers and streams where natural insects are less abundant.

Rainbow Trout *(Oncorhynchus mykiss)*

Current Records
British **24 lb 2 oz 13 drm (10.965 kg)**
World **42 lb 2 oz (19.1 kg)**

Season
April to September but all year round in some stillwaters.

Distribution
Stocked in many rivers and stillwaters. Spawns in Derbyshire rivers.

Natural Diet
Daphnia, caddisflies, mayflies, fry and midges.

Top Spots
Midland reservoirs such as Grafham and Rutland Water.

Top Tip
Fish a sunk lure in reservoirs.

Recognition

The rainbow trout is the most important and widely distributed of all the salmonidae species. It is a hard-fighting fish capable of making repeated runs and leaps – a fact which has not gone unnoticed by anglers. Although once known as *Salmo gairdneri,* it has recently been reclassified as *Oncorhynchus mykiss* to show its close relationship with the various Pacific salmon species, such as the coho and chinook.

Most rainbows live and breed entirely in freshwater both in rivers and lakes and, depending on the strain and location, are extremely variable in their colouration. Many wild fish are quite heavily marked with a profusion of dark spots over their body and fins. On our own reservoirs rainbows that have reached the peak of condition on a diet of small invertebrates and fish are bright silver and similar in appearance to steelhead of North America and Canada. Typically though, most rainbows have a dark, greenish-grey back and pale belly with a pink stripe running from the gill plate and along the flanks, the intensity of which increases as the trout comes into spawning condition. Two notable exceptions to this are the golden trout and the blue trout, although both are simple colour morphs of the rainbow developed by fish farmers and stocked in various UK waters.

Habitat and Location

The rainbow trout's original range includes North America, from Alaska down the western seaboard as far as southern California, and Mexico's Pacific coast, Canada and north-east Asia. Also owing to its ease of rearing and the fact that it tolerates lower water quality and higher temperatures than the brown trout, it has been introduced to many other parts of the world including Europe, Australia and New Zealand, along with South America, Africa and India. Additionally, in certain parts of the world, notably its home range of North America and Canada, there is a sea-run form of the rainbow trout known as the steelhead.

Like the sea-run brown trout the steelhead spends most of the time feeding in the ocean only returning to a river to spawn. Steelhead grow large, up to 20 lb (9.07 kg) or more, and when newly returned to freshwater they are bright silver, extremely strong and one of the most prized sporting fish. They can be caught on a range of tactics including bait, fly fishing and spinning.

ABOVE: A beautifully conditioned rainbow taken on a lure from Hanningfield, a reservoir in Essex.

Behaviour and Feeding Habits

The rainbow trout's diet is extremely varied, and along with a range of aquatic invertebrates and insect larvae, it is not averse to eating larger creatures such as grasshoppers, fish and even mice. In the wild, rainbow trout can grow to 50 lb (22.7 kg) or so, but this is exceptional, and the average is much lower, with a 5 lb (2.27 kg) specimen being a good one. On the smaller put-and-take waters, which often stock big farmed fish, it is possible to catch rainbows in excess of 10–20 lb (4.54–9.07 kg), and the "cultivated" record in the UK stands at over 36 lb (16.33 kg). On reservoirs where the initial stock size is only 1–2 lb (0.45–0.9 kg) a double figure rainbow is the fish of a lifetime, although one water, at Hanningfield in Essex, has produced grown-on fish of over 20 lb (9.07 kg).

Being a cultivated fish, in the UK, there is no specific season for rainbow trout, and a number of waters are open to anglers all through the year. However rainbow trout still come into spawning condition, the female fish becoming dark and full of eggs while the males develop a pronounced kype. In such condition these fish are not good to eat and so some farmers produce triploids, using heat or shock on the eggs to alter their genetic make-up. This produces sterile fish which remain in good condition throughout the year.

Although the vast majority of rainbows caught in the UK are

produced in fish farms, there are a few waters where introduced fish sustain a natural population. The Derbyshire Wye is a prime example where rainbows were first introduced in 1912-13 and have since established themselves, so now "wild" rainbows of up to 2 lb (0.91 kg) or so can be caught in that river along with the brown trout and grayling.

Rainbow trout can be caught on bait, spinner and fly, although, due to restrictions imposed by most fisheries, fly fishing is the most widely used method. On rivers and small lakes normal nymph, wet-fly and dry-fly tactics work well. They also work

extremely effectively on the larger reservoirs. However, rainbows are a shoal fish, and it is necessary to locate the depth of the shoal to be successful. In reservoirs some interesting feeding patterns have developed. Although the bulk of their diet comprises chironomid larvae and pupae during early and mid summer, rainbows will feed heavily on daphnia, a tiny animal plankton that proliferates in many of the richer lowland waters.

Rather than picking off the daphnia one by one, the trout swim through the swarms scooping up this living soup and, as it is such a high-protein food source, rapidly put on weight and improve in condition. When rainbows are feeding this way they will often take brightly coloured flies and lures – orange is a great favourite – as long as they are fished at the same level as the daphnia.

LEFT: A fry-feeding rainbow from Grafham Water showing the superb condition of many fish that are taken from the rich waters of the lowland reservoirs with plentiful feeding.

ABOVE: The lucky angler plays a rainbow taken at the Avon Springs fishery. Most waters have a day limit of four to eight fish.

BELOW: Playing a rainbow hooked from a boat on the Eyebrook reservoir, near Corby in Northamptonshire.

Grayling *(Thymallus thymallus)*

Current Record
British **4 lb 3 oz (1.899 kg)**

Season
June to March.

Distribution
Patchy. Clear, shallow and fast chalk streams in southern England, Yorkshire and the north west.

Natural Diet
Insects, small crustacea, fish fry and water snails.

Top Spots
Southern chalk streams, the Avon, Test and Frome; the Yorkshire rivers and the Welsh Dee.

Top Tip
In best condition in winter in clear water. Fly fish with Red Tag or when trotting; hold back the float occasionally to make the bait rise to just under the surface.

Recognition

The grayling cannot be mistaken for any other fish. It is a very beautiful fish with a huge, sail-like dorsal fin, and a silvery-blue streamlined body with delicate violet stripes. Grayling also have irregular dark spots on their flanks, as unique to each specimen as fingerprints are to a human being. As a member of the salmonidae family, the grayling has an adipose back fin, which is a small fleshy protuberance situated between the dorsal and the top lobe of the deeply forked tail. The head is delicate, being small and pointed, and the mouth contains very tiny teeth with which it grips its food. They also have the scent of wild thyme, hence their Latin name, and make very good eating.

Habitat and Location

The large dorsal is intended to help the grayling to combat very fast flows, and this is the favoured environment of the species. They abound in clear, shallow, unpolluted chalk streams, happily co-existing with trout. Unfortunately, those beautiful fish are very sensitive to water pollution levels and as a result they are not widespread, living in pockets. The southern chalk stream tributaries of the Hampshire Avon and the Kennet, as well as the main rivers themselves, support a thriving population, as do some of the shallow, colder, faster-flowing streams of the north-east and north-west, and grayling are present in the border rivers of Scotland. Elsewhere, particularly in the Midlands, good grayling fishing is very hard to find.

Small to average grayling live in the shallow, fast glides in large shoals, with the bigger fish tending to hang on the creases between the fastest flow and more sedate water. The real specimens, as with other fish, are usually found in steadier, deeper water, where they do not need to expend so much energy and can live a lazier life.

LEFT: **A good grayling being brought to the net, caught on a wet fly in autumn. Grayling are often classed as coarse fish and caught trotting maggots and worms down a swim.**

Size

Grayling do not reach great sizes, and any fish over 1 lb (0.45 kg) in weight is a very worthwhile fish and a 2 lb (0.91 kg) sample a specimen. It is a rare angler indeed who has taken grayling over 3 lb (1.36 kg) in weight, and the current record of 4 lb 3oz, (1.89 kg) taken in 1989, will take an awful lot of beating.

Behaviour and Feeding Habits

The grayling's natural diet consists of small crustacea, nymphs, water snails, fish fry and any spent insects that drift by. They feed on the bottom but are quite happy to feed higher in the water during hatches of nymphs and mayflies. They group up in large shoals and, unlike roach, dace or chub, the coarse fisherman is unlikely to be able to entice them into a swim by regular feeding. Once they colonize an area they stick with it until they are ready to move on. The angler is well advised to spend time checking where they are feeding before contemplating fishing for them.

Grayling feed throughout the year but are at their best in very cold conditions, those clear, icy winter days when perhaps only dace are also willing to feed. In these conditions, they form very tight shoals and individuals tend at times to flash or splash at the surface. These are the signs to look for before starting to fish. Grayling are avid fly feeders, and all the methods appropriate for small river trout take their share of grayling. Leaded nymphs fished singly or a team of rolled nymphs are favourite methods of presentation but in the right conditions they will take the floating fly avidly and in the winter the Red Tag is the traditional pattern to try, fished either wet or dry.

If you want to fish a swim for grayling using coarse fishing methods shoals of grayling will respond to the stimulus of a regular supply of drifting maggots and casters; and trotting a float is the most enjoyable presentation. Initially, the grayling will often feed hard on the bottom but gradually feed at all depths as the competition for the loose feed warms up. This often will not apply to the biggest fish in the shoal, who will hang back and intercept any food item that trickles along the bottom past the rest of the shoal. These bigger fish are lovers of worms, and it is a good idea periodically to swap the maggot for a good-sized worm and run the float further downstream of the normal catching area.

Grayling of all sizes are always looking for aquatic nymphs shooting to the surface, and will often respond savagely to a trotted hookbait made to behave in the same way, by holding back the float so that the bait swings up in the water. Takes to this presentation can be dramatic.

TOP: **A dry-fly fisherman plays a good grayling from a very thick bank.**

ABOVE: **Two good grayling caught trotting.**

BELOW LEFT: **The huge dorsal fin of the grayling shows clearly in the water.**

BELOW: **When autumn comes and the leaves start to change colour the grayling fisher comes into his own.**

Equipment

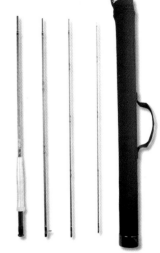

Game fishing rods fall into three main groups. Fly rods, spinning rods and bait rods. However, it is fly rods which come in the greatest variety, in a wide range of lengths and line weights designed to fish different-sized waters and fly sizes. They also come in two types. The majority are single handed and used for most types of trout, grayling and, where the water is small enough, salmon fishing too. The second type, which are double handed, are designed primarily for fishing for salmon on large rivers such as the Spey, the Tweed and the Tay. These long powerful rods, up to 16 ft (4.88 m)in length, can cast the heavy lines needed to cover a big river along with handling a large fish in a strong current.

9 ft 6 in (2.9 m) travel rod

Rods

Single-handed Fly Rods

7–8 ft (2.13–2.44 m) Lightweight rods that are used mostly on smaller streams and rivers where long-distance casting is not necessary. They are ideal for dry fly and nymph fishing, where their lightness make them perfect for the light tippets and tiny flies that are needed.

Typically line weights are in the AFTM 3–5 range, although it is possible to find rods capable of casting as low as a 1 weight line for extreme delicacy. For the light-line fanatic, an American rod manufacturer has built the ultimate rod, capable of casting a 0 weight line. It is so light that a line and reel have had to be made especially to match it.

8–9 ft (2.44–2.74 m) Trout rods of this length are normally rated to cast lines between AFTM 5–7. This makes them very versatile, able to cope with a wide range of conditions and water types. Those at the lighter end of the range are ideal rods for dry fly and light nymph work, while those capable of casting a 6–7 weight line are perfect for trout fishing on medium to large rivers as well as lakes and reservoirs.

9¹/₂–10¹/₂ ft (2.9–3.2 m) These longer rods include the more powerful models used for distance casting on stillwaters or where a river is large and the current strong. At the lighter end of the range they are ideal for fishing anything from a dry fly to heavyweight nymphs, while the heavier rods, designed to cast lines 8–10 weight, are ideal for distance casting or when big fish are the aim on stocked waters. These rods will fish floating or intermediate lines perfectly, but also have the power to fish fast-sinking lines and big flies so often used on reservoirs.

11–12 ft (3.35–3.66 m) Although the longest single-handed rod used, this type of rod is not necessarily more powerful than those in the 9¹/₂–10¹/₂ ft (2.89–3.2 m) range. The reason is that it is designed primarily for loch-style

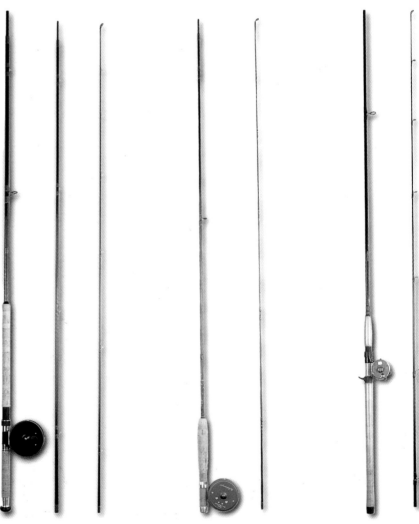

14 ft (4.27 m) salmon rod with reel

7½ ft (2.29 m) trout rod with ultralight reel

Bait rod with baitcaster reel

fishing from a drifting boat. The technique involves casting a relatively short line, up to 10 yds (3 m) or so, from a drifting boat, and this style of casting requires a more through-actioned rod. As a result, loch-style rods are normally designed to cast lines rated AFTM 5–7.

Double-handed Salmon Rods

11–16 ft (3.35–4.88 m) Unlike the shorter single-handed rods, double handers range from 11–16 ft (3.35–4.88 m). The shorter, lighter models, capable of casting a 6–7 weight line, are designed for fishing a floating line when the river is at summer level and small flies are the most effective. The longer, more powerful rods are designed for when the river is running high at spring or autumn levels and heavy lines and big flies are required to cover the water. Rods such as these, capable of casting 10–11 weight lines, are necessary when large heavy flies, such as metal tube flies, are being fished deep on a sinking line.

Travel Rods

With anglers increasingly prepared to travel to far-flung corners of the globe, multi-sectioned travel rods are becoming more popular. Their appeal is obvious. There is no longer the need to travel with a cumbersome two-piece rod that needs to be transported in a special tube, when a multi-sectioned rod will pack away safely in a suitcase. Today, modern rod manufacture is so good that a rod of five or six sections will perform just as well as one with only two. Many anglers are switching to travel rods for all fishing.

Spinning Rods

Spinning rods come in a range of sizes and weights, depending on the size of fish being sought and the weight of spinner or plug that needs to be cast. Some models of spinning rod are available with a standard reel seat for when using a

8 ft (2.44 m) trout rod with ultralight 6 reel

fixed-spool reel or with a finger which allows the angler a better grip on the rod when using a multiplier.

For light spinning for trout an 8–9 ft (2.44–2.74 m) rod is ideal. It should be capable of casting weights as low as 10 g or less. For sea trout and salmon on small- to medium-size rivers the rod should be 9–10 ft (2.74–3.05 m) and designed to cast weights up to 40 g. For larger rivers you need a rod 10–11 ft (3.05–3.35 m) long capable of casting weights up to 50–60 g with the power to cast large spinners and plugs and hold big fish in fast water.

Bait Rods

For bait fishing on small trout rivers a lightweight coarse fishing or spinning rod is more than adequate, but for worm and shrimp fishing for salmon something longer and more powerful is required. Many anglers use a rod 12–13 ft (3.66–3.96 m) long, designed to cast weights in the 10 to 50 g range. The extra length helps control the bait in its path downstream.

Reels

Game fishing reels can be broken down into three main groups: fly reels, multiplying reels and fixed-spool reels. Fly reels, as their name suggests, are used solely for fly fishing. Multiplying reels are used mostly for spinning for salmon. Fixed-spool reels, on the other hand, are not only used for spinning but are also ideal for bait fishing either with worms or prawns.

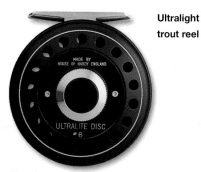

Ultralight trout reel

Fly Reels

Unlike other types, a fly reel is only wound when a fish is being played or when line is rewound prior to moving position; otherwise the line is left hanging in coils from where it is repeatedly cast. For this reason fly reels are sometimes considered merely to be line holders. This is a dangerous assumption because when a big fish that is determined to run is

Standard salmon reel

hooked a poorly designed reel is a liability. The simplest and cheapest fly reels have only a simple ratchet mechanism to prevent the spool from running free and the line unwinding unnecessarily. While this is fine for small fish or where a fish cannot run far, for big fish, or where light lines are being used, a smooth free-running drag is essential.

Although uncomplicated in overall design and construction, most modern fly reels have a sophisticated and very effective drag mechanism. These mechanisms come in a variety of forms but the most common is a disc drag, a circular pressure plate which acts on the spool and which can be increased or decreased in its intensity by a control usually found on the back of the reel. By tightening and loosening the drag, various strength tippets can be used without the constant fear of a break, although the angler should always remember to adjust the drag to the line strength being used before fishing because it is difficult to fine-tune during the fight.

The importance of a smooth, effective drag is at its most obvious when the fisherman is playing a big or hard-fighting fish on light lines. Without one, any jerks and rapid runs made by the fish could easily snap a delicate tippet or leader. Even when strong lines are used for big fish, such as salmon, a drag that will tighten down hard but still allow the line to run out smoothly will make playing the fish a great deal easier while increasing the angler's confidence.

Reel showing the line guard

Most fly reels are single actioned. This means that, unlike a fixed-spool or a multiplying reel, there are no gears, so each full revolution of the handle makes only one turn of the spool. This makes rapid line retrieval a problem and can only be counteracted by having a large central arbor so that as much line as possible is wound back on every revolution. This is the reason why fly reels should always be filled to their full capacity, the fly line being supported by plenty of backing.

Trout reel

The size of fly reel used depends on the rod and line. The volume of a size 10 double taper, of the type used for salmon fishing, is much greater than a 5–6 weight used for trout, and so the reel has to be correspondingly larger. Also the rods themselves vary greatly in weight, so an 8 ft (2.44 m) brook rod balances best with a tiny 2$\frac{1}{2}$ in (6 cm) diameter reel weighing around 3$\frac{1}{2}$ oz (90 g), while a 15 ft (4.57 m) double-handed salmon rod requires something near 4 in (10 cm) in diameter – weighing in at a hefty 9–10 oz (250–275 g). To make sure the angler has the right size reel for the job most manufacturers give a line capacity with the reel's specification, and this includes the amount of backing that needs to be added first.

Grey Marquis reel

Multipliers and Fixed-spool Reels

A small multiplying reel, a 6500, is the standard for spinning for salmon and big trout, having the capacity to take 250 yds (228 m) of 15–20 lb (6.8–9.07 kg) breaking strain nylon. The smooth, powerful drag mechanism of the multiplying reel is

Multiplier reel

especially important when fishing for large salmon in a fast-running river. It allows the angler to apply great pressure on the fish – to help tire it – but still gives line easily if the fish makes a run. As ultra-long casts are rarely needed the level wind is never removed, as it sometimes is for saltwater fishing. This ensures that the line is always laid smoothly and evenly along the spool, preventing the line from bedding in to itself under the pressure of playing a big fish.

Although fixed-spool reels can readily be used for spinning, for game fishing they are at their most effective used in conjunction with baits such as worms and prawns. Because the line can be fed from the spool much more easily with the fixed-spool reel, it allows the bait to be worked with the current. Some models are particularly good because the spool can be left to run free, allowing line to be paid out until the bait has worked through the area being fished or a fish has actually taken. A turn of the reel handle disengages the bait-runner mechanism, allowing the bait to be rewound or a fish struck.

3010 fixed-spool reel

Fly Lines and Leaders

Originally fly lines were produced from real silk dressed with linseed oil to keep them supple and afloat. Today much of the hard work has been taken out of fly-line maintenance by modern plastic polymers which produce lines needing only the occasional clean to keep them performing at their best.

Fly Lines

Modern materials and manufacturing processes have also produced a further benefit: the ability to create fly lines of widely varying profiles and densities, allowing the fly fisher to present a fly in ways and at depths never before possible.

Fly lines are now available not only in floating, intermediate sinking and medium-fast sinking rates but in

Windcutter fly line

ultra-high density also, with which the fastest sink at a rate of almost 1 ft (30 cm) per second is enough to fish effectively in very deep or fast-flowing water.

For most fly fishing a floating or intermediate-sinking line is the most widely used. Intermediate lines are effective allowing the fly to be fished a few feet below the surface – just where the fish are cruising. Recently, clear lines, such as the "slime line", have become popular.

In addition to the various single densities of fly line there are also sink tips. These lines have a floating belly and running line with a short section of sinking line at the front. They enable a fly to be fished a few feet down in the water while the bulk of the line floats on the surface. The advantage of this is that although the line fishes like a sinker it can still be mended on the surface or allowed to drift on surface currents if fishing a stillwater with buzzers.

The two main profiles for fly lines are double taper and weight forward. Double-taper lines have two tapers of equal length on either end of a central belly. This is the traditional profile, most effective for short- to medium-distance work – up to 20 yds (18.23 m) or so – and where accuracy and delicacy are the main requirements. Weight-forward lines, on the other hand, have most of their weight concentrated in a 12 yds (11 m) belly at the front end of the line. This belly slims down at its rear into much thinner running line. This running line shoots easily through the rod rings, allowing the weight-forward line to be cast long distances. For this reason weight-forward lines are the optimum choice when medium- to long-distance casting is the main requirement. As a compromise, long belly lines with a longer front taper are now manufactured which, over short distances, cast with a delicacy similar to a double taper but which can also be cast much longer distances by launching the belly in the air first, allowing the thin running line to be shot.

For long-distance work a third type of line, the shooting head, is the most effective. Here a short, heavy section of fly line, 10–12 yds (9–11 m) in length, is connected to a slick shooting line such as braided or monofilament nylon. It allows casts of over 40 yds (36.58 m) to be made and is popular for reservoir lure fishing.

Tippets or Leaders

Unlike most other types of line, such as monofilament nylon and Dacron, that require additional weight to cast them, fly lines contain the required weight to load a fly rod. But since the fly line has to be very thick and conspicuous to do this, a finer, more delicate material is needed to link the fly line to the fly in order not to frighten the fish. This is known as the leader or tippet. Leaders come in many forms from straight or tapered mono-filament nylon to braided nylon or polypropylene, or special composites such as Poly Leaders: these are available in varying sink rates and act as extensions to the fly line itself.

Most basic of all is a leader of straight monofilament nylon. Where leader turnover is not vital or where it is assisted by a breeze, plain monofilament is a cheap and easy

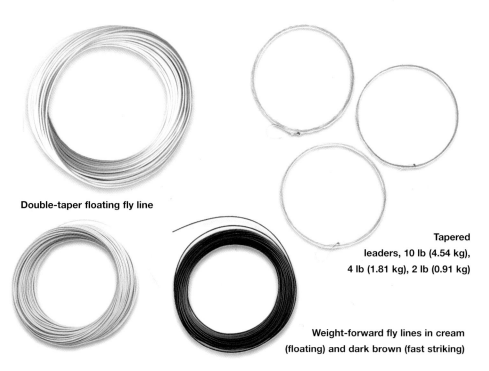

Double-taper floating fly line

Tapered leaders, 10 lb (4.54 kg), 4 lb (1.81 kg), 2 lb (0.91 kg)

Weight-forward fly lines in cream (floating) and dark brown (fast striking)

alternative to more complex systems. Also where well-spaced droppers are being used, such as when stillwater nymph fishing or fishing loch-style, it offers the most effective leader construction.

Various breaking strains of nylon are used but for stillwaters 4–6 lb (1.81–2.72 kg) leaders are the most generally used. Although relatively expensive, co-polymer nylon and fluorocarbon are becoming increasingly popular with anglers because they are less visible in the water than ordinary nylon.

For most dry-fly work or where the fly is to be fished on or in the water's surface, a simple tapered nylon leader is ideal. This transfers energy from the fly line through its length, helping the fly to turn over properly even into a breeze. The leader's taper goes from thick at the butt to thin at the tip. An extra 2–3 ft (60–90 cm) of fine nylon tippet is then added at the tip so that repeated fly changes or other damage does not require the replacement of the entire leader.

Braided nylon leaders perform a similar function, though because they are braided some anglers maintain that the energy of the cast is transferred more efficiently to the fly. That apart, the benefit of braided leader is that by altering its density – achieved by adding fine lead or copper wire when it is being manufactured – it can be made either to float or to sink at varying rates. The latter offers great advantages in getting a fly down to fish that are

lying well below the surface while keeping control of a floating line.

Poly leaders are a recent innovation in leader design. They are manufactured as short-tapered lengths of fly line attached by a loop to the tip of the fly line, so offering the best energy transfer of all. They come in a wide range of densities, from floating and intermediate sinking to slow sinking, plus a range of fast sinkers. They can be attached either to a floating or any other density of fly line, providing many alternatives when it comes to fly presentation.

Backing

This is the strong thin line of approximately 30 lb (13.61 kg) breaking strain that is wound on to the fly reel before the fly line. Backing performs a twofold function, keeping the coils of fly line as large as possible – which prevents tangling – and, more importantly, acting as a reserve of line should a hooked fish run out more than the 30 yds (27.43 m) of fly line on the reel.

Backing comes in many forms but the most popular two are braided nylon – not monofilament – and braided polyester. The latter is the most often used because it is cheaper than braided nylon and is also thinner, thus allowing a greater amount to be wound on to the reel. This has advantages when using a small lightweight reel but not where big fish, capable of making long runs, may be encountered; then braided nylon may be the better choice.

Sundries

Along with all the major items of tackle such as rods, reels and clothing there is a variety of other sundry items which, if not vital, are certainly a great help at the waterside.

Landing Net

Having hooked your fish the next task is to land it safely. From the bank it may be possible to beach a played-out fish, but from a boat this is not an option and the answer is to use a landing net.

A landing net has many advantages. For example if you are going to release the fish it can be guided into the net before it is so tired that recovery would be difficult, while if the fish is going to be kept it is less likely to be lost if it is netted quickly. There are many designs for trout and salmon landing nets. For salmon the sturdy, metal-framed Gye net is large enough and strong enough to handle a big fish.

For trout, a lighter model, with a telescopic handle, makes landing a fish easy even from a boat. When choosing a net consider the size of the fish you are likely to catch. Finally, remember that the mesh should be knotless – knotted mesh landing nets are now illegal.

Tackle Bag

This is used to carry all those odds and ends, such as spare reels and fly boxes, which are needed for a day's fishing. They vary in size from spacious ones large enough to hold the multitude of tackle required for reservoir boat fishing to light compact versions used for rivers and streams. Most are made from cotton duck, which is perfectly strong enough, while the fittings vary from brass and leather on traditional models to modern plastic snap locks. Whatever the type of bag, look for one that is strongly built, preferably lined to keep the tackle dry, and with a wide adjustable shoulder strap.

Fly Boxes

As you build up a collection of flies you need somewhere safe to put them. Fly boxes are the usual places and they come in a wide range of sizes and with a variety of methods for holding the flies in place. For lures and wet flies simple foam-filled boxes made from wood, plastic or aluminium work well. Recently the plastic Fox box with its gripping slots, which prevent moisture rusting the hooks, has become very popular. For dry flies a rigid aluminium box with a number of small compartments, is the best choice because it prevents the delicate hackles being crushed.

Line Tray

If you wade deep while fishing a sinking line you will find that on the retrieve the backing sinks beneath the water's surface to the extent that it makes shooting the line very difficult. Even if you manage it the extra drag will reduce the casting distance. So rather than letting the line simply fall into the water, placing it into a line tray ensures that it shoots easily.

It is worn around the waist and on each pull of the retrieve the line is allowed to fall into it.

Priest

If you intend to dispatch your fish – and on some waters releasing fish is not allowed – it is important to do so quickly. The most efficient method is to use a priest (for administering the last rites). This is a heavy wooden or metal implement used to strike the top of the fish's head. Some priests come with a combined marrow-spoon. These are ideal for finding out what a fish has been eating.

Wading Stick

Fishing for salmon often involves wading in a deep powerful river. However confident you might feel, the use of a wading stick will help ensure you keep your footing even in a strong current. It is used to brace the angler against the flow and help feel for any potholes. Various models of wading stick are available, the most complicated being the collapsible type. The best is a simple, solid stick with a good strong handle and a heavily weighted end to help keep it firmly planted on the river bed.

Boat Seat

Fishing all day from a boat can be uncomfortable. A simple cushion will help but the real answer is to use a purpose-made cushioned boat seat with a back to give plenty of support. Many designs are available that either fit over the gunwales and can be adjusted, depending on the width of the boat, or simply clamp on to the thwart boards. While a fixed seat is quite adequate, one with a swivel, which allows the angler to turn while seated, makes handling the engine or pulling in the drogue far easier.

Bass Bag

If you intend to take fish to eat, it is important to keep them as fresh as possible. A simple method is to use a bass bag. These are made of straw, or other water-absorbent material, and are soaked with water before placing the fish in them. The evaporation of the water produces a cooling effect which helps keep the fish fresh, so they must not actually be left in the water – as on a warm day the fish will slowly poach. A better method is to place the fish in a cool box complete with ice packs. For larger fish, special lined cool bags are available that take the same frozen packs as a cool box.

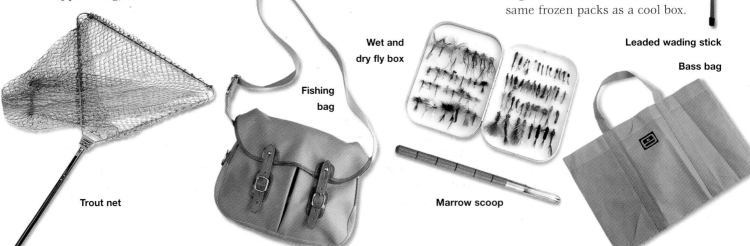

Wet and dry fly box

Fishing bag

Leaded wading stick

Bass bag

Trout net

Marrow scoop

Clothing

Angling is often done in bad weather. Game fish in particular have a requirement for cool, well-oxygenated water and usually take better when the weather is poor. This means that the angler is often fishing in cold and wet conditions. From a boat the situation is even worse; with nowhere to go if the weather turns nasty, the angler simply has to brave it out.

Waterproof Clothing

Fly fishing is an active pursuit, and to be comfortable the angler needs to be kept warm and dry even in the most inhospitable conditions. So, for anyone serious in their fishing it is important that they have the right clothing. At one time waxed cotton was the principal waterproof material, but modern breathable fabrics, such as Goretex and Ventex, are becoming increasingly popular and are now the most widely used. The fact that they are both lightweight and extremely waterproof makes modern breathables the ideal choice for game fishing. They have a number of advantages. For example, their lightness doesn't impede casting and, unlike waxed cotton, they do not become uncomfortably stiff in cold weather. Also the fact that they breathe, allowing sweat to pass out through the membrane while preventing rain from getting in, ensures that the wearer

Waterproof jacket

remains comfortable with none of the dampness and condensation that is so often a problem with other materials such as PVC or waxed cotton.

Waterproof trousers for boat fishing

For boat fishing or when deep wading is not required a three-quarter length coat with a built-in hood is perfect for even the toughest conditions. This design of coat is long enough to keep the angler's back dry even in the heaviest rain and with a suitable fleece underneath will keep the wearer warm, too. This is the length of coat to wear over thigh waders or when fishing from a boat, combined with a pair of waterproof trousers of the same material, to keep the legs dry.

When choosing a waterproof coat look for reputable makes, all of which have good design and properly taped seams to ensure that their products don't leak. It is also important that there is a secure flap over the front of the zip to stop any rain being forced through, plus efficient storm cuffs to prevent any water running down the arms when they are raised while casting.

When deep wading it is advisable to wear a specially designed wading jacket. Again manufactured from a breathable material, these jackets are cut short so that they stay clear of the water. However, as they are much shorter than normal, this style of jacket should always be worn with chest waders. And, as with other waterproof coats, there should be a spacious, built-in hood, preferably with a peak, to prevent rain dripping into the eyes and running down the back of your neck.

Waders and Boots

For fishing either from a boat or when walking in the shallow margins of a lake or river, ordinary Wellington boots are quite adequate. However, many anglers need to wade that bit deeper, especially when fishing from the bank on large lakes and reservoirs or on rivers. Thigh waders are perfect for this task, allowing the angler to wade comfortably in water about two feet deep, giving access to spots unreachable without them. Most thigh waders are made from flexible rubber with a boot attached. Depending on where the angler is fishing they may be cleated – making them ideal for rough ground – studded or felt-soled, which, though smooth, provides the best grip on slippery rocks when they are covered with algae.

For deep wading, so often necessary on rivers when fishing for either trout or salmon, it is vital to use chest waders of which there are three main types. Most commonly used are membrane waders made of PVC or nylon that have a flexible body and legs with an integral rigid boot. They have the advantage that they are relatively cheap, if a little heavy. An advance on the ordinary PVC wader is the breathable wader. These, too, are a membrane but a breathable one constructed to allow sweat but not water to pass through – keeping the

Thigh waders

Chest waders

wearer dry from both sides. Though quite expensive they are becoming increasingly popular and are perfect for summer use or when a lot of walking is involved.

However, when wading for long periods in cold, deep water, neoprene rubber waders are the best choice. They are 3–5 mm thick and made of the same material as divers' wet-and-dry suits. They have tremendous insulating qualities that help keep the angler warm even in the depths of winter. Also, being soft and flexible, they are extremely comfortable suffering none of the pinching that can be a problem with thin, membrane waders. Neoprene waders are available in two types. The first has integral boots, while the second is stocking-foot with additional lace-up boots that look similar to ordinary walking boots. While waders with built-in boots are quick to get on and off, those that use separate boots provide better ankle support – a definite advantage when walking long distances down the river bank.

Safety

Apart from comfort, which is important when wading deep in chest waders, it is vital to consider the safety aspect. Always take great care, especially on unfamiliar rivers, and if you have a ghillie always take his advice over the safe areas to wade. In addition it is important to use an automatically inflating life-jacket should the worst happen. Most important of all, don't wade too deep, especially where the current is strong and, if needed, use a wading stick for support. Even after taking these precautions it is always better to back off into shallower water and cast that bit further than to wade so deep that you lose your footing.

Life-jackets

With game anglers often fishing from boats or wading deep in powerful rivers, safety is very much an issue, and for this reason inflatable life-jackets are becoming increasingly used. Modern life-jackets are a far cry from the old cumbersome foam-filled ones that put off many anglers. Today, automatically inflated jackets are light and unobtrusive, slipping easily over the neck and arms.

TOP: Flotation waistcoat.

ABOVE: A waistcoat specially designed to take the equipment needed by fly fishers.

A small carbon dioxide cylinder connected to an automatic mechanism is used to inflate the jacket should the angler fall into the water. With a buoyancy of around 150 Newtons the wearer floats easily, face up, even when fully clothed. For those wearing neoprene chest waders more buoyancy is needed and a jacket with 200 Newtons of lift is required to counteract the effect of the waders.

In addition, for those who like to wear a fishing waistcoat, some manufacturers produce combined life-jackets and multi-pocketed waistcoats that are quick and easy to slip on and offer the same buoyancy as the standard life-jacket.

Waistcoats

For anglers who like to walk long distances when they are fishing, a waistcoat or fishing vest takes much of the strain out of carrying all the extra tackle and odds and ends needed at the waterside. Instead of putting all this paraphernalia into a fishing bag and then carrying it around the neck a waistcoat allows enough gear to be carried, but it is evenly distributed around the shoulders thereby causing far less strain. Multi-pocketed waistcoats are available in a wide range of models, from standard cotton ones to lightweight mesh versions which, though having fewer pockets, are ideal when deep wading is necessary and a longer more complicated model would only get wet.

When choosing a fly-fishing waistcoat decide what type of fishing you will be doing most, then find one with enough pockets to carry all you need. This should include pockets for spare spools, fly boxes, leader material etc, plus a large pocket in the back to hold a folded waterproof. If you do a lot of wading or boat fishing it is worth considering a waistcoat with a built-in life-jacket, thus necessitating the purchase of one garment rather than two.

Thermal Fleece

While the system of layering clothing might be new to the angler, it is one long practiced by walkers and mountaineers who need clothes which are light and waterproof but also very warm. These are exactly the same requirements as the angler's, and with more manufactures of angling

Peaked cap

Tweed hat

clothing designing garments with this in mind there is no longer any reason to be cold and wet. A breathable waterproof coat worn over a fleece makes a perfect combination for even the worst weather. Fleeces come in a range of designs from simple single layers, either with a zip front or as a pullover, to those with a Goretex lining, which makes them windproof.

Underwear
For very cold conditions long thermal underwear and a long-sleeved vest of fine silk or Capilene may be worn under trousers or fleece pants along with a rollneck top. This provides the first in a system of layers which trap the air and also draw any moisture away from the body keeping the wearer dry, comfortable and warm.

Gloves
In very cold conditions it is important to keep your hands warm. Fly fishing, in particular, requires constant manipulation of the line both to make the fly work properly and to detect takes. With numb fingers this ability is obviously impaired. The only real answer is to use some form of protection such as gloves or mittens, and the best are those specially designed for anglers where the fingertips can

ABOVE: The well-equipped flyfisher in summer with broad brimmed hat and polarizing glasses.

be left uncovered when fishing, so the line can be easily felt while the rest of the fingers and the hands are kept warm. Although absorbent materials should be avoided, some of the modern ones are so good they provide reasonable warmth even when wet, although two or three pairs can be a boon if you are fishing for salmon early in the year on a really wet day.

Hats
Various types are used by anglers, from the traditional flat cap and deerstalker to wide-brimmed bush hats. For summer wear a light, long-peaked cap to protect the eyes from the sun's glare and help the angler

spot fish beneath the water's surface. With a hood, this style of hat may even be worn during the winter, although in very cold conditions something warm such as the traditional deerstalker with flaps that can be pulled over the ears prevents excessive heat loss.

Polarizing Glasses
As a further safety measure, if you are not a spectacle wearer it is important to wear a pair of polarizing glasses. These not only prevent any possible injury from a fly being cast, but they also stop the sun's reflected glare from the water damaging the eyes. A secondary benefit is that they also help the angler see beneath the surface of the water.

BELOW: Casting for a trout in summer.

Fleece fishing mittens

Casting

The key to presenting the fly to the fish is the cast and this can take various forms depending on the type of fly fishing you are doing and the area being fished. In fly casting the rod acts as a spring while the fly line provides the weight to load the rod – no leads or other weights are used. The main types of cast used by trout and salmon anglers are the overhead cast, the roll cast, the double haul, and the Spey and double Spey casts, with the horseshoe and steeple casts being used when circumstances dictate. Casting is itself a source of great pleasure and satisfaction and it contributes greatly to the enjoyment of fly fishing.

ABOVE: Casting a dry fly upstream.

The Overhead Cast

The standard overhead cast is the basic cast for the beginner to master. It is used over short distances where accuracy rather than distance is important. For a right-handed fisher the angler stands, right or left foot forward according to preference, with 5–6 yds (4.57–5.03 m) of line on the water and the rod held in the right hand, pointing towards the water. Gripping the line with the index finger the forearm is brought smoothly upward until the hand is to the side but just in front of the face. With the wrist remaining straight the rod is now stopped at the 11.30 position so it is upright and slightly behind the angler. (This figure of 11.30 refers to a clock face, with 12 o'clock being directly above the angler's head, and acts as a guide to the correct rod position at any stage of the cast.)

The backward sweep of the rod loops the line out behind the angler and flexes the rod. At this stage it is important not to let the rod drop back too far because this will collapse the cast. With the hand still in the 11.30 position a pause is made to allow all the line to extend fully behind the angler. The pause is crucial and its duration depends on the length of line being cast. Once the line has extended at the back the rod is then brought forward to the 1.30 position. This "loads" the rod and causes the line to loop out in front of the angler. The rod is then dropped to the 2.30 position, thus allowing the line's momentum to "shoot" any slack out over the water.

If greater distance is needed this process is repeated on each forward stroke with a little line being paid out until the required amount is outside the tip ring. The technique is known as "false casting" and it is used by dry fly fishers to dry the fly and place the cast. The line is then shot as before.

Making an Overhead Cast

1 This angler has his weight on his right foot and has started to drive the line out across the water. Note the tension in the rod as the line starts to come forward.

2 The rod has reached the forward position. The tension has left it and the angler will "shoot" the line trapped by his left hand as the cast extends across the river.

The Roll Cast

The roll cast is the simplest of all presentations. Where a back cast is obstructed it can be the only way of presenting a fly, although accuracy and distance are limited. With the rod pointing down, and a short distance of fly line on the water, the rod is lifted upright then laid back over the shoulder so that the line forms a large loop behind the angler. Once the line has reached this position the rod is swept forward in a single smooth action. The loop of line plus the drag of the line on the water flexes the rod so that by punching it forward and down, the line is made to roll straight out over the water. This gets the fly on to the water and is an ideal method for lifting a sunk line from the water prior to a normal overhead cast.

Making a Roll Cast

1 This cast can be made with trout and salmon rods. Here a trout angler is using a roll cast on a lake.

2 The rod is brought back to the right and then swept up to the vertical position making a loop of line on the angler's right. The rod is then "cut" down to the water and the loop is rolled out across the surface.

ABOVE: Casting an upstream nymph on a north-country stream into the fast water at the head of a pool.

LEFT: Fishing a dry fly on a north-country river. Here the angler has his weight on his left foot and is casting a short line with his cast thrown well up behind him. Accuracy is much more important than distance when fishing for trout in this type of water.

The Double Haul Cast

The double haul is the standard technique for long-distance casting with a single-handed rod in which a haul on the line is made both on the forward and back cast. This action generates much greater line speed allowing the line to be shot long distances once the optimum amount of line has been launched into the air. The haul is made with the free hand, which is allowed to drift upward towards the butt ring before making a quick downward haul at the beginning of both the forward and back casts. The line is shot as usual on the forward stroke once 10–15 yds (9.1–13.7 m) of line are outside the tip ring, any loose coils of line on the ground being carried with it. The double haul is the usual technique for reservoir trout fishing because it enables a full fly line, 30–35 yds (27–32 m), to be cast.

Single Spey and Double Spey Casts

When using a double-handed salmon rod and an overhead cast is impossible, the Spey and double Spey casts come into their own. Based on

LEFT: The start of a double haul. The line is pulled sharply downwards as it is picked off the water and the left hand is then allowed to drift up to the butt ring. The angler makes another haul as the forward stroke is made; this is quite difficult to time correctly and the reservoir angler must practice until it becomes second nature. The two hauls make the line travel much faster through the air and give great distance to the cast.

the roll cast the Spey cast takes plenty of practice to become proficient at it, but most competent salmon anglers should take the trouble to master it. The timing of each stage is crucial as the line must be in contact with the water to load the rod and create the final forward cast. Too late and the line will lift off the water, and the power will be dissipated.

The single Spey is ideal for a strong downstream wind when the angler runs the danger of hooking himself in the back of the neck with the standard overhead cast. The angler faces downstream and raises the rod slightly towards the near bank. The rod is then swept away smoothly out and up, with the butt pivoting at the angler's belt buckle. As the rod comes round to the roll cast position the line will come off the water and be swept upstream with the last 4 yds (3.66 m) touching the water's surface. The rod is then punched forward and high so that the line and fly loop out over the water. It is essential that the fly is drawn upstream so that it is level in the water with the angler. This enables

the angler to change the direction of the line and cast the fly across the river rather than just downstream.

The double Spey is different from the single Spey and is performed over the shoulder of the bank from which the angler is fishing. Fishing from the right bank it is made over the right shoulder and conversely over the left shoulder when fishing from the left bank. It is most useful for changing the direction of a large heavy fly, and an expert can cast a very long way indeed using this cast. If fishing from the right bank the rod is swept slowly back-handed upstream in front of the angler so that the fly comes to rest about 5 yds (3.66 m) in front of the angler. The rod is then rolled out and round downstream in a figure-of-eight movement, and the rod is lifted back up over the right shoulder into the roll cast position. Finally, the rod is punched forward, shooting the line and fly out over the water. It is essential that the loop made in the line is as close to the line as possible, "shaving the cheek of the line", and it is possible to shoot a great deal of line when using this cast. It does, however, take a good deal of practice to perfect.

The Horseshoe Cast

This is a useful cast to use fishing for salmon in a very strong downstream wind if you do not want to use the single Spey cast. When the cast is fished out, lift the fly off the water back-handed, over the left shoulder – fishing from the left bank– and then bring the fly back round over your

The Single Spey Cast

The angler pulls the line upstream until the fly is level in the water. The rod is then lifted over the angler's right shoulder and the loop rolled out across the river in a continuous movement. With practice this cast can be done quite fast and with a good deal of force.

RIGHT: **The angler is making a roll cast to clear the fly before casting again. This is similar to the single Spey but can be made off either shoulder.**

right shoulder in one continuous movement. It is not possible to cast a very long way using the horseshoe cast but it makes a neat finish and avoids the fly and line getting wrapped round your neck.

The Steeple Cast

This is a cast to use when you have a very steep bank behind you, or some other obstacle, and you cannot use the single Spey or double Spey cast. It can be made with both trout and salmon rods. With a salmon rod hold the rod out in front of you with your hands rather wide apart on the butt, and the right hand (if fishing over your right shoulder) as far down the rod as you can reach. Raise the rod sharply upwards, throwing the line high into the air behind you. When the line is fully extended bring the rod down and forward, and this pushes the line out over the water. If you are carrying out a steeple cast with a single-handed rod, it is important not to cock your wrist but hold it out stiffly as you bring the rod up. It is surprising how this cast helps you avoid even the most awkward of banks behind you.

RIGHT: **The angler is completing a double Spey cast off the right shoulder. The line is just picking up from the water. Experts can cast a long way using this technique.**

The Double Spey Cast

The river flows from left to right. The first movement is back-handed, pulling the fly upstream. The rod is then brought over the right shoulder and a loop of line formed on the right. Next, the rod is cut down across the river, shooting the line and fly out across the water. The dotted lines indicate the movement of the rod tip in diagrams both above and opposite.

Salmon Fishing

Salmon fishing has been called the greatest of all sports, and with some justification. Nowadays the Atlantic salmon is under grave threat from netting both on the high seas and in river mouths. Catches in rivers are much reduced, and on many rivers strenuous efforts are being made to implement catch-and-release policies to preserve the spawning stock.

Fly Fishing for Salmon

Salmon can be caught on fly, spinner, worm and prawn, but for the majority of dedicated salmon fishers, fly fishing is the best and most effective way, and on many rivers the rule is fly only. Even on rivers such as the Wye, the famous Welsh salmon river, many beats have now banned the use of spinner and bait.

There are two main ways to fish for salmon with a fly. The first is when the water temperature is cold in the early and late months of the year, below 48°F (9°C): then the technique is to fish with a large fly 2 in (5 cm) or more and to use a sinking line. Later in spring and summer when the water temperature rises above 48°F (9°C) smaller flies fishing on floating lines are the most effective way.

Depending on the river you are fishing the same tackle can be used for each method. Standard tackle when fly fishing for salmon includes a double-handed 15 ft (4.57 m) rod designed to take a 9 to 11 weight line. This type of rod is powerful enough to cover a large river like the Tweed or Spey and works well with either an overhead or Spey cast. In the summer or fishing on smaller rivers, any rod from 12–14 ft (3.66–4.27 m) will be perfectly adequate depending on the water you have to cover.

You need a reel to balance the rod that will hold the line and 200 yds (183 m) of 30 lb (13.61 kg) backing. Modern reels have interchangeable spools, one to hold a sinking line and one to hold a floater. You need a leader of nylon of between 20–8 lb (9.1–3.63 kg) breaking strain, depending on the height of the water and the time of the year that you are fishing, and salmon flies in a variety of sizes from 3 in (7.5 cm) down to size 8 or 10. Salmon have been caught on minute trout flies, and it is a common mistake to fish with too large a fly. Popular modern patterns include Willie Gunn, Ally's Shrimp, Munroe Killer, Stoat's Tail and Tadpole, although there are countless salmon flies and the old patterns are more colourful, with more romantic names, such as Green Highlander, Mar Lodge and Lady Caroline.

Fly fishing for salmon is really a scaled up version of classic down-and-across wet fly fishing. The line should be cast downstream and across the current so that the fly swings enticingly across the pool. When the cast is fished out the angler takes one or two paces downstream and casts

again. That way the whole pool is covered systematically. You can leave the line to work naturally with the current or work the fly by pulling in a little line at a time to make the fly dart across the current as if it was a small fish. Takes can come at any time, but most often they occur as the swing begins or at the end when the fly is "on the dangle".

There is something rather special about catching a salmon on the fly. The best chance is when the water conditions are right, the air is warmer than the water and the river has begun to run clear after a spate.

Alternatively, there are three other methods of presenting the fly to the salmon. The first of these is to "back up" a pool immediately after it has been fished in the orthodox manner. When doing this the angler starts at the tail, cast fairly square across the current, and then takes three or four steps upstream, at the same time steadily pulling in the line. This sweeps the fly over the fish in a continuous curve. A good even bank is a great help when attempting this form of fishing.

The other two methods are really summer tactics: the first is to fish with a bushy dry fly, such as a Rat-faced Macdougall, and cast continually over one fish for several hours. This can goad the salmon into taking. It works best when the water is over 60°F (15°C). The other is to "dibble" a large fly down a run, fishing it half out of the water; tubes are now available that will fish at half-cock. Another way of dibbling is to fish with two flies and bounce the dropper on the top of

the water. Fishing with a dry fly, strike as soon as you see the rise, but when dibbling wait till the salmon has taken the fly down before tightening – this requires great self-control.

Spinning

On some rivers when the river is running high spinning is the preferred option. During the early season when the river is still swollen by winter floods, a large spinner such as a Toby, a yellow-bellied Devon Minnow or one of the deadly rubber-tailed spinners can be very effective when fished steadily through a pool. The spinner is cast across and downstream then allowed to sink for a second or two before engaging the reel. How far across stream the cast is made and the weight of the spinner used depends again on the strength of the current. Tobys come in varying sizes and weights up to 28 g. Devon Minnows and Rapalas require additional casting weight in the form of spiral leads or Wye leads. At least one or, better still, two strong swivels should be used to prevent line twist.

Tackle for salmon spinning includes a 10–11 ft (3.05–3.35 m) spinning rod, capable of casting weights up to 2 oz (50 g), and a fixed-spool or multiplier reel loaded with 250 yds (228.6 m) of 15–20 lb (6.8–9.07 kg) nylon.

Bait Fishing

The most commonly used bait for salmon is the humble worm, either large lobworms or smaller brandlings. Depending on just how powerfully the

ABOVE LEFT: Fishing for salmon in summer on the River Spey.

ABOVE: An angler spinning on the River Tay, Scotland, in spring.

river is flowing these can be fished either singly or in bunches. The worms are attached to the hook with lead shot or a drilled bullet connected to the line for casting and sinking the bait to the bottom. The most effective and skillful method of fishing a worm for salmon is to cast it upstream and allow it to bump gently along the bottom just slower than the current.

Tackle for worm fishing includes a powerful 12 ft (3.66 m) rod combined with a fixed-spool reel loaded with 250 yds (228.6 m) of 10–15 lb (4.54–6.8 kg) breaking strain nylon. A single size 4 to 8 hook, often with a sliced shank to help retain the worm, is tied to the end with large split shot either pinched on the line or fished as a fixed leger. How much shot is used depends on the strength of the river.

Another effective bait for salmon is shrimp or prawn, although its use is banned on many rivers as it disturbs the water for other forms of fishing. Shrimps are available in a variety of colours, both natural and dyed, with red and purple being the most popular. To fish them they are first straightened out, then a pin is pushed down their middle. A treble hook is then inserted and the whole thing bound together with elasticated thread. Shrimps can be fished in the same way as the worm or, where allowed, fished under a float.

Sea Trout Fishing

There are two main types of sea trout waters. First, those rivers that have large runs of sea trout, and second, some lochs or lakes connected to the sea by a short river that are renowned for their sea trout fishing. Among the best-known sea trout rivers are the Welsh rivers, the Irfon, Teifi and Conway, the West Country rivers, the Torridge and Tamar, and a number of the Border rivers on the west coast of Scotland. The best-known lochs are probably Loch Maree and Loch Hope in Scotland.

What to Take

There is sometimes no apparent reason why one river will have good runs of sea trout while another has relatively few. All salmon rivers have some sea trout but on some there are so few that they are not worth a special expedition, while a nearby river may have a fair number.

The type of fishery dictates the style of fishing. On most sea trout rivers the main fish are taken at night, after dark, while on lakes and lochs, the main fish are caught in daylight. It must be remembered that in June and July in northern Scotland particularly, night has a short duration.

The tackle required for fishing a river depends very much on its size. Generally, for fly fishing, on a reasonably large river, you will need a 9½–10½ ft (2.9–3.2 m) single-handed

ABOVE: A fine fresh sea trout taken from the River Conway at night.

rod capable of casting a 7–8 weight line. A rod suitable for fishing a large reservoir is ideal. The leader should be a minimum of 7–10 lb (3.18–4.54 kg) breaking strain, and you need both floating (or floating with a sinking tip) and slow-sinking or intermediate lines, on separate reels or reel drums. You will need a variety of sea trout flies, not just the old favourites such as Teal, Blue and Silver, and Grouse and Claret, but also any flies that are particularly favoured on the water you are going to fish, and a number of lures, both for fishing on a sunk line after midnight, or cork-bodied floating lures for use on the surface.

As well as rod, reel, nylon and flies, the night fisher for sea trout will need waders, a wading stick, net, a bag for keeping any fish, midge-repellent, scissors, priest, spectacles (if worn), and finally and most importantly a good torch with fresh batteries that is not going to dull to a dim glow at 1.30 am on a dark night.

Night Fishing

Night fishing is not something for the uninitiated, and the beginner is urged to solicit the company of a local or companion who knows the river and the tactics to follow on their first visit. If you are in the position of going fishing alone at night on a new river, it is essential to walk down the river in daylight first, examine all the pools, choose where you hope to fish and then wade the pools when you can see. Also cast to where you think the fish are likely to be and if necessary mark your line with a dab of luminous paint, or check off and memorize the amount of line you

BELOW: A good sea trout is netted on a dark night. A companion is a good idea when fishing at night, particularly on a strange river.

have pulled off to reach the lie. At night sea trout often move up and down streamy runs as they feed or drop back to the flats at the tails of deep pools where they have been lying under cover during the day.

Fish a team of two, not three flies: two is less likely to tangle than three; and fish normal wet fly down the pool to start with. If nothing has happened by midnight, and the regulations of the river allow you to fish on, change to a sunk line and try fishing a sunk lure. Another tactic at night when you can hear the sea trout splashing on the surface is to switch to a floating lure, cast across and down so that it drags across the surface of the water leaving a wake.

Often this is a method that catches the bigger fish. However, it is worth stating that few rivers are the same and local knowledge is invaluable.

Fishing Stillwaters

Fishing on stillwaters for sea trout is very different. The preferred method on many waters is to dap with a bushy fly. You need a longish rod 11–12 ft (3.35–3.66 m) that ideally should be quite soft, a reel, and some floss line. The technique is to cut off a length of about 15 ft (4.57 m) of floss line and then make a series of overhand knots down the line. This just holds the line together a bit which is necessary otherwise the fibres fray too much. Attach a short 4 ft (1.22 m) leader of 7–8 lb (3.18–3.63 kg) with a

dropper to the floss line and attach the floss line to the reel line. Tie the bushy fly on the dropper and a standard sea trout fly, such as a Grouse and Claret, on the point.

When you start to fish, and some wind is absolutely necessary, pull off all the floss line and then let it just blow out in front of the boat, forget about the point fly and bounce the bushy fly along the tops of the ripple in front of the boat. The point fly is only there to anchor the dropper that otherwise can be uncontrollable in a strong wind, although sometimes fish will take the point fly. Fish often come to the dapped fly with a tremendous splash, and it requires nerves of steel not to snatch the fly away too quickly – concentrate on the dapped fly intently and wait for the fish to take it down before tightening.

It is normal for one rod in a boat to dap while the other fishes with a team of wet flies. It is the duty of the wet fly fisher to keep out of the way of the dap, although he should cover any fish that moves to the dap if the dapper fail to connect.

Sea trout can also be caught on a dry fly in still conditions. Cast out and give the occasional twitch, using a team of wet flies. In this situation, a floating line fishing the flies just under the surface is normally best.

Bait and Sea Fishing

In rivers, when the water is high, sea trout can be caught during the day on the fly, and spinning and fishing with worms or maggots is often successful.

Sea trout can also be caught in the sea. This can be very profitable, and the best conditions are places where there are stillwaters close to the sea connected by short streams or burns when the water is low in summer. Then the fish congregate off shore and can be caught by casting with fly or light spinners such as a mepps, during the two hours on either side of high water. It can be quite surprising hooking a good sea trout in the open sea and the main danger is losing it in the weed around the rocks. Another good place is a tidal pool on a river where a worm can be very successful.

Sea trout are fickle creatures. They have been much under threat over the last twenty years, and their numbers have declined markedly; infestation by lice from salmon farms and commercial netting of sandeels have been blamed. Now some famous sea trout waters hardly hold any fish at all. It must be hoped that this situation changes and conservation measures are successful, for hooking and landing a large sea trout at night or having one lunge at the dap is a thrilling experience.

ABOVE: Dapping on Loch Hope, one of the famous sea trout lochs in Sutherland.

BELOW: Fishing a small sea trout river during the day. Sometimes when the small sea trout, usually known as sewin or herling, run in they can be stalked in daytime and caught by fishing a small dry fly upstream. This can be very exciting on light tackle.

Dry Fly Fishing

For many anglers dry fly fishing is the pinnacle of the sport. In bygone days it was regarded as an art so difficult that only a few privileged anglers could attempt it. Nowadays fishing with a dry fly is relatively commonplace and is practised both on rivers and stillwaters. Nevertheless it remains a fascinating way of fishing. To find a rising fish, identify the insect the trout is feeding on and cast to that fish, then watch your fly in breathless anticipation as it floats downstream towards the trout; then to see it rise in the water and take it down off the surface is a wonderful experience, one that is treasured by all anglers.

ABOVE: A blue-winged olive dun on bankside vegetation. This fly hatches in the evening and is one of the best for the evening rise.

River Fishing

Successful dry fly fishing depends on a good hatch of aquatic insects such as upwings or caddisflies, or a fall of terrestrials (land-based insects blown on to the water). When this occurs fish switch from feeding on nymphs and crustacea to taking flies off the surface. The essence of dry fly fishing is to imitate a small creature as it floats on the water. Some patterns such as those incorporating Cul de Canard feathers, which are naturally impregnated with oil, float well untreated but most need an application of floatant to prevent them becoming waterlogged. Floatants come in two main forms, either as a spray or a gel, and are applied sparingly so they do not clog the fly's delicate hackles.

The predominant group of insects of interest to anglers on rivers are commonly called upwings or mayflies. They are members of the family Ephemeridae. There are a number of species, including the blue-winged olive, the medium olive, iron blue and the mayfly, and they make up a large part of the diet of trout and grayling. Trout take them from the surface at two stages in their development. The first is when the nymph first hatches out as a dun, or sub-imago, and floats downstream until its wings have dried and it can fly away. Many duns have greyish wings and olive or pale-straw coloured bodies. After one or two days the duns become sexually mature and change into the imago, or spinner. Males and females mate in the air and the females return to the water to lay their eggs and die. When they have finished laying their eggs they float downstream with their wings outstretched in the form of a cross and are known as "spent". Spinners frequently have reddish bodies, long tails and gauzy wings..

The normal method for fishing a dry fly in a river is to use a single fly on a tapered cast. Accuracy is more important than distance, and the tapered leader, which transfers the energy of the cast and helps it turn over properly, allows the fly to be placed exactly in front of a feeding fish. The successful dry fly fisher spends a great deal of time observing the water, checking the flies that the trout are taking and reading the current to see whether there is any likelihood of the fly dragging and scaring the fish when it is cast.

During the summer months the rise is likely to be to a species of upwinged dun. These olive-coloured flies are quite easy to identify drifting downstream like miniature sail boats. If this proves to be the case, a size 14 or 16 CDC Dun is a good imitation to use. If it is impossible to tell what is causing the activity a more general pattern such as the Adams or the Hare's Ear, again in the same sizes, makes a good starting point.

The next step is to position yourself almost opposite the fish but slightly downstream, making use of any bank-side vegetation to keep out of sight of the fish. The cast should be made so that the fly lands just

LEFT: Fishing the dry fly on the River Avon, Hampshire. The angler has used the bankside vegetation for concealment and is casting at a trout across the river.

upstream and directly in line with where the fish is rising. The fly is then allowed to drift into the fish's vision and, if pattern and presentation are right, the trout gently sips the imitation down. What is important is that the fly drifts with the current like a real insect. If the line drags the fly will skate across the surface and be refused. Casting upstream helps but casting a snaky line, so that there is some slack, ensures that the fly can drift without drag for long enough to fool the fish.

Tackle for river dry fly fishing includes a rod 8–9 ft (2.44–2.74 m) long, teamed with a 4–6 weight floating double taper or long belly fly line. The leader is of tapered nylon 9 ft (2.74 m) long tapering to a 3 lb (1.36 kg) breaking strain tippet. Effective flies include the Adams, Hare's Ear, CDC Dun and Greenwell's Glory.

Stillwater Fishing

Once considered a fringe technique, today dry fly fishing is regarded as one of the most deadly methods on stillwater. Apart from a few specific imitations such as those of the daddy-longlegs (crane fly) and the lake olive, stillwater dry flies look quite different from river patterns. They rely as much on teased out body materials as hackles to keep them floating, and many are designed to sit low in the surface film. Many patterns including the Bob's Bits imitate a hatching

RIGHT: **Dry fly fishing on the River Frome, Dorset. Many south-country rivers have a timeless quality with lush green banks and leaves stirring in the breeze.**

chironomid midge – the predominant insect on lakes and reservoirs everywhere.

Stillwater dry flies are usually fished, either from a bank or boat, as a team of three, or as a mix with a dry fly on the top and middle droppers and an emerger pattern, such as a Suspender Buzzer, on the point. In calm conditions or when trout are being selective a single fly is effective fished on a short tapered leader with a fine tippet of 4 lb (1.81 kg) breaking strain. The tapered leader allows accurate casting helping to present the fly right in the path of a cruising fish. However the fly is fished, it should be treated with floatant and the leader rubbed with a degreaser to make it sink. This prevents the telltale disturbance caused by a leader trapped in the surface film.

ABOVE LEFT: **A good trout rises to a blue-winged olive making the characteristic kidney-shaped whorl in the water.**

ABOVE: **Fishing a dry fly upstream in fast water. Good eyesight and accurate casting are a great help in these conditions.**

For stillwater dry fly fishing a 9–10 ft (2.74–3.05 m) long rod matched with a 6–7 weight forward, floating line provides both distance and accuracy. When fishing a team the leader is 12 ft (3.66 m) of 5 lb (2.27 kg) breaking strain nylon with two droppers spaced 4 ft (1.22 m) apart. Typical fly patterns include Bob's Bits and Hoppers in various colours plus the CDC Dun during a hatch of lake olives. An imitation crane fly or adult damselfly is also effective when the naturals are on the water.

Nymph Fishing

By definition nymph fishing means presenting a fly to a fish beneath the surface, for a nymph is the immature stage of an aquatic insect and spends its life underwater. To be accurate a nymph is the pre-emergent stage of insects such as mayflies, damselflies or stoneflies, which ascend to the surface of the water and there change into the first stage, or sub-imago, of their winged existence. However, fly fishers often use the term nymph more generally, to describe any aquatic invertebrate, be it a nymph, larva, pupa or even a crustacean such as a shrimp.

ABOVE: A natural pond olive nymph starting its ascent to the surface.

Upstream Nymph

The key to fishing a nymph is presenting it as naturally as possible, mimicking the way a real insect moves. On rivers this usually means fishing the nymph upstream and allowing it to "dead drift" with the current. When a real olive nymph or a shrimp is disturbed, rather than swimming it will usually just drift with the current for a short distance until it can regain cover.

It is possible to fish a nymph down-and-across wet fly style, but it is not a way to catch the better fish. To fool the larger, more wily fish the most effective and tested methods are the upstream nymph and the rolled nymph.

In upstream nymphing the line is cast up-and-across-stream so that the flies drift back to the angler at the same speed as the river is flowing.

Also, because the line isn't dragging them around across the current they sink to the fish's level and drift downstream like a real nymph. To keep in contact with the flies, the line must be retrieved – not to feel a take but to ensure that when one comes there isn't too much slack line, and the angler can strike properly.

While the technique of upstream nymphing is straightforward, the real skill comes in detecting takes. Because the line is slack, takes are not going to be felt. In clear, smooth water this is not a problem. By using polarizing glasses to cut out any surface glare, the fish can often be seen taking the nymph – the angler seeing a flash of white as the mouth opens and closes. However where the surface is broken, or where the angle and level of the light makes seeing fish impossible, another method is

required. Instead of looking for a fish the angler watches the end of the line intently. As the line drifts back with the current it does so at a steady, unhindered pace. It is only when the nymph catches the bottom or when a fish takes that the line will stop and drag under the surface. Deciding which is which takes experience, but the best way of determining the difference is that a take usually produces a sudden stab of the line or it moves across rather than with the current. If it is weed or the bottom the line simply draws steadily under. This is not a perfect rule, and usually any twitch or hesitation in the line's drift should be met with a strike.

To make the tip of the fly line more obvious it can be painted with fluorescent orange paint, or a fluorescent orange or yellow braided loop can be used to attach the leader. For fishing at longer range a sight bob, or strike indicator, is a great advantage. Made from a buoyant material such as polystyrene, a sight bob is attached to the leader a few feet above the nymph. It also helps control the depth the nymph fishes.

Rolled Nymph

Similar to the upstream nymph is the rolled nymph. Developed by Czech and Polish anglers, the technique is being used to great effect in the UK for both trout and, particularly, grayling. It involves fishing a team of heavily-weighted nymphs on a very short line, the nymphs being "rolled" along the river bottom almost under

LEFT: Nymph fishing on the River Wye in Derbyshire.

RIGHT: Nymph fishing on the River Avon, Hampshire. Nymphing trout are easy to see in the clear water of the chalk streams.

the rod tip. Instead of just casting, the angler wades carefully until little more than a rod's length from the area to be fished.

With only a short length of fly line and the leader outside the tip ring the nymphs are flicked directly upstream, and as the current carries them back the nymph on the point sinks until it is tripping along the bottom. As the nymphs drift through the slot being fished the rod follows their progress keeping in contact all the time. When the flies are directly below the angler the rod is lifted or the line retrieved and recast.

Takes can come throughout the drift and are detected either as a draw on the line or more usually by it pausing in its normal drift. The end of the drift is particularly productive and fish will often take when the nymphs are directly below the angler and beginning to rise in the water.

Tackle

Ideal tackle for the upstream and the rolled nymph is a rod 8½–9½ ft (2.59–3.05 m) long, rated for a 5 to 6 weight line. The line itself is always a floater, which can be brightly coloured, either orange or yellow, to help detect takes.

For the upstream nymph the leader is 8–10 ft (2.44–2.74 m) long and of tapered nylon. Tippet strength varies depending on the size of nymph being fished and for standard size 12–16 hooks it is 3–5 lb (1.36–2.27 kg) breaking strain. One or two nymphs may be used, the second lighter pattern being fished, either on a short dropper or attached to the bend of the larger, heavier nymph by 6–12 in (15–30 cm) of nylon. Effective patterns include the Pheasant Tail Nymph, Hare's Ear and Iron Blue.

Since the rolled nymph has to get down to the fish's depth very quickly, the patterns used are large and heavily weighted. The leader is also quite short – no more than the length of the rod on to which are tied three nymphs or bugs, two on evenly spaced droppers. Size 10 nymphs are standard for this technique, as are patterns such as the Hare's Ear and shrimp, which are weighted to make them sink.

Nymph Fishing in Stillwaters

Nymphs are also used widely on lakes and reservoirs, and for much the same reason as on rivers – their ability to produce better-than-average fish. Most stillwater trout fisheries in the UK are artificially stocked, mostly with rainbow trout along with a small proportion of brown trout and occasionally some brook trout. On reservoirs and larger lakes the trout are normally stocked weighing about 1 to 1½ lb (0.45–0.68 kg) and fish larger than this have grown-on by feeding naturally on a diet of crustaceans, insects and small fish.

When fish have been feeding on natural insects for some time they can become quite selective in their diet, and rather than taking any fly or lure drawn past their nose they require a more imitative approach.

The most common natural food for stillwater trout is the larvae and pupae of the chironomid midge. Fishing an imitation, especially of the pupa, is one of the most effective methods of catching fish in stillwaters. Midge larvae live in the bottom silt of lakes and reservoirs, and when pupation occurs these pupae must rise to the surface to transform into the winged adult.

Small vulnerable creatures such as midge pupae make easy pickings, and reservoir trout eat them by the hundred. The pupae can be taken anywhere from the bottom to the surface, and one of the most successful techniques is to fish three pupae imitations, hanging them from midwater to the bottom. This is done by using a floating fly line and an ultra-long leader, in excess of 20 ft (6.1 m), with two droppers spaced 4–6 ft (1.22–1.83 m) apart. All three patterns should be designed to sink quickly but the heaviest of the three is fished on the point so that it gets to the bottom as rapidly as possible.

The method can be used from either boat or bank, but as it is dependent on moving the flies very slowly the weather needs to be quite calm, especially from a boat, which needs to be anchored to keep it stationary. From the bank, water 8–15 ft (2.44–4.57 m) deep is best, which usually means fishing from a headland or a dam wall where the water is normally deeper close-in to the shore. Once the line has been cast the flies are then allowed a few seconds to sink down through the water before starting the retrieve.

Another method is to fish the nymph just below the surface film when the natural insects are hatching.

RIGHT: A beautiful wild brown trout taken on a nymph. The white line makes the take easier to spot.

Wet Fly Fishing

Wet fly fishing is the traditional method of fishing for trout and grayling in fast-flowing rivers of the north and west of the country where the hatches of insects may be sparser, and the dry fly is more difficult to present to a feeding fish. It is common particularly in the north of England and Scotland where a specific style of wet fly fishing has developed. Many game anglers started fishing for trout with a wet fly in small streams and burns as young children using a team of three flies, casting them across and downstream and waiting for the pluck on the line as the trout intercepted the flies in their path across the river. On stillwaters a number of methods have developed over the years to catch trout in reservoirs as well as the traditional lakes and lochs.

ABOVE: **Fishing the River Wharfe, Yorkshire, with a wet fly in early spring.**

Wet Fly Fishing on Rivers

On rivers the standard method for fishing a wet fly is known as down-and-across. This means that the line is cast downstream at an angle across the flow and involves the angler casting, and allowing the flies to fish round in the current before taking a pace downstream. The process is then repeated so that gradually a stretch of river or a pool is fished thoroughly and every inch of the water is covered.

When fishing down-and-across the flies are fished just under the surface and the angler must try and keep the line as straight as possible so that he or she can strike immediately when a trout rises to the fly or a pluck on the line is felt. The cast is made at an angle across and down the river and the flies are made to swing across the path of a fish. The method is very effective, especially on rain-fed rivers where the fish are opportunistic in their feeding.

It is important to be in control of the line at all times. In a river that is flowing quickly it is easy to have the flies whipped around in the current far too fast. Fish will still be caught but they will be fewer and almost certainly smaller than if the flies are fished at a steadier pace.

In a river that is moving slowly the line can be cast at less than 45° to the flow and allowed to come round naturally. However, to reduce the effect of a fast current the line should be cast at more than forty-five degrees to as much as ninety degrees, all depending on just how fast the river is moving. The speed of the river needs to be judged and the flies made to swing only slightly faster than the current. To help this happen an upstream mend is made. This is done by raising the rod, parallel to the water and placing the line back upstream with the tip of the rod immediately after the cast is made. This helps to take the belly out of the line and makes the flies fish round more steadily.

The effect of the belly on the current is the same as that used by a water-skier. Water-skiers use the fact that they can actually go faster than the boat that is pulling them by swinging across its path. We need to ensure that the opposite happens and that the flies move almost at the same speed as the river – just as any natural food item would. The only exception to this comes right at the end of the swing. With the line almost directly downstream of the angler it can go no further and the flies rise to the surface. As they do they accelerate a little and often a fish will make a grab as its potential food "tries" to escape.

Takes can come anywhere during the cast and are normally felt as a simple tightening of the line. If just a

LEFT: **Down-and-across on a typical north country river.**

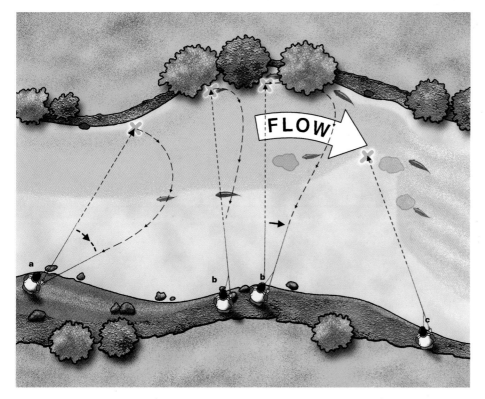

Wet Fly Fishing

The angler at (a) is fishing the head of the pool in the traditional down-and-across manner. If the current is deep enough the flies can be allowed to come right round under the angler's bank before a new cast is made. It is most important to keep the line as straight as possible when fishing in this style.

The anglers at (b) are fishing across-and-down in the Tweed-style and casting again when the flies have travelled a short distance. This method is especially good when fish are feeding under trees on the far bank, as the angler can float the flies down to the fish.

The angler at (c) is fishing the tail of the pool upstream with a team of wet flies to avoid scaring the fish present in the shallower water. When fishing this type of water look out for ripples on the surface: this indicates the presence of larger rocks that the trout will shelter behind. Make sure that all the potential lies are thoroughly covered.

quick pluck is felt and the fish has not taken the fly properly the flies should be allowed to keep working, because the fish will sometimes come back for a second go. A simple lift of the rod is enough to set the small hook if the fish hasn't already hooked itself against the drag of the line.

For normal river wet fly fishing for trout and grayling a rod of around 9–9$\frac{1}{2}$ ft (2.74–2.9 m) long is ideal. It should have a medium-to-through action to absorb the shock of any sudden takes and be capable of casting a number 5–7 line. The smaller and less powerful the river the lighter the tackle can be. Normally a floating line is used, though if the current is particularly fast a sink tip line or a sinking polyleader can be effective because it prevents the flies from skating across the surface.

Although a single fly can be used, it is common practice to fish a team of three on a leader about 9 ft (2.74 m) in length with the flies spaced on droppers 2–3 ft (0.61–0.91 m) apart. The breaking strain of this leader should be about 3–5 lb (1.36–2.27 kg), though it can be lighter if the water is very clear and the fish are proving difficult.

Effective flies for this style of fishing include the Hare's Ear, March Brown, Partridge and Orange, Woodcock and Orange, Snipe and Purple, and Black Spider tied on hooks from size 12 to 16. Usually it is

the smaller, sparser patterns that are most productive. In some rivers, particularly the River Tweed, and the Border rivers, where the angler is fishing large pools, the most effective style is to cast a team of wet flies or nymphs across river, allow them to drift downstream a short distance and then cast again. The flies are not allowed to swing down and across with the current. This is a good method to use when the fish are feeding on hatching nymphs as it allows a natural presentation in the same way as a dry fly. If the flies are drawn in slowly before the next cast is made, then the fish often takes at this point, similar to the "induced take" of

the chalk stream trout when a nymph is drawn past its nose by the fisher.

Wet flies can also be used in the same way in the tails of pools where the water is shallower and the angler would run the risk of scaring the fish if he fished downstream in the traditional manner. A good method is to cast upstream and draw the flies down-and-across over the fish.

BELOW: Fishing the Upper Severn in early spring. The wet fly is at its most productive in the early part of the year when fly hatches are sparser and the trout are starting to come back into condition after spawning. Soft-hackled spider patterns are preferred.

Wet Fly Fishing on Stillwaters

On stillwater the methods of fishing wet flies are a little different from those used on rivers, because without the benefit of a flowing river all the movement imparted to a fly comes from the angler.

Traditional Loch-style

When boat fishing the most popular traditional technique is known as loch style. This method has its roots in fishing for wild brown trout on the lochs of Scotland and loughs of Ireland. The anglers fish from a boat drifting sideways-on to the wind. In such a position the boat provides a stable platform for two anglers and possibly a boatman to work down the wind covering the fish-holding areas of the water. On big, natural lakes the most productive water is often quite shallow, 2–8 ft (0.6–2.44 m) deep, and involves the boat being worked with the oars around the shoreline, the fringes of islands and close to rocky outcrops.

Traditionally loch-style involves "short-lining" in which the angler casts no more than 10 yds (9.14 m) in front of the boat and retrieves a team of wet flies back through the wave. Intrinsic to this technique is working the top dropper on the top of the waves at the very end of the retrieve. It is an effective technique because fish that are following the flies will often take the top dropper fly as it is dibbled by gently lifting the rod.

BELOW: **Wet fly fishing on Rutland Water. This is one of the modern reservoirs that has helped to advance the techniques of wet fly fishing on stillwaters.**

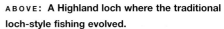

ABOVE: **A Highland loch where the traditional loch-style fishing evolved.**

Fishing Modern Reservoirs

Although traditional loch-style is still widely used the method has been adapted for fishing the lowland reservoirs of England, Wales and Scotland. Instead of just fishing a floating line various densities of sinking lines are used to cover all water depths. Reservoir trout, particularly the rainbows, feed on creatures such as midge larvae and pupae and daphnia – a tiny animal plankton. Daphnia in particular are very sensitive to light, and the sunnier it is the deeper they go. So, in order to catch trout effectively on reservoirs it is important to be able to locate their feeding depth. This is done by fishing a team of wet flies on a sinking line exploring the various levels until takes are forthcoming.

Unless there is obvious activity on the surface the usual method is to start with a fast sinking line such as a Hi-D or a Di-7. Cast out up to 30 yds (27.43 m) in front of the boat, and allow the line to sink before starting the retrieve. By counting down the line can be left longer and longer until the flies hit the bottom, at which point it is obvious that they are working at all depths.

Retrieve rates can be varied from a steady figure-of-eight to a fast strip bringing the flies right up to the boat. At this point it is normal to hang the flies for a few seconds before recasting, because trout will often follow a fly close to the surface before taking, so pulling the line off too quickly will miss these fish. When a take comes it is then a matter of deciding how deep the fish was. If it comes on the first few pulls it is likely that it was close to the bottom, so simply carry on. However, if it was quite close to the boat it could be worth changing to a slower sinking line such as a Wet Cell II or even an Intermediate, especially if the situation repeats itself.

If a hatch of midge takes place and fish can be seen feeding on the surface it is well-worth switching to a floating line. Basically the flies should always be fished at the trout's feeding level – never too deep, never too close to the surface. Although wet flies work from an anchored boat the usual technique is to allow the boat to drift on the breeze – covering a great deal of water and a great many fish. However, in a very strong wind the boat can drift too quickly to fish the flies effectively. In these circumstances a drogue is used.

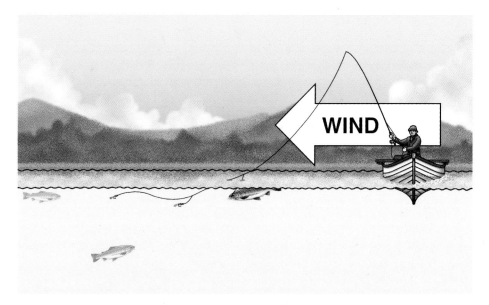

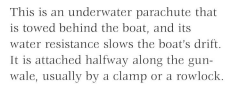

This is an underwater parachute that is towed behind the boat, and its water resistance slows the boat's drift. It is attached halfway along the gunwale, usually by a clamp or a rowlock.

Tackle

Tackle for traditional loch-style fishing includes a medium-actioned rod 10–11 ft (3–3.35 m) long, capable of casting a 6–7 weight line which is usually a floater. Leader length is 10–15 ft (3–4.50 m) of 5–7 lb (2.3–3.2kg) breaking strain nylon. This leader is normally tied with two droppers spaced 3–4 ft (0.91–1.22 m) apart enabling a team of three flies to be used. For reservoir use the set-up is similar but rods tend to be faster actioned and slightly heavier, especially for sunk-line work. Here a rod of 10–10½ ft (3.05–3.2 m) matched with a 7–8 weight line is the most popular combination. Leaders are normally longer, 12–18 ft (3.66–5.49 m), with the droppers 4–6 ft (1.22–1.83 m) apart, particularly if the water is deep.

Flies include the Silver Invicta, Doobry, Soldier Palmer, Bibio, Peach Palmer, Oakham Orange, Mallard and

ABOVE LEFT: Dibbling the top dropper on a reservoir. Dibbling works best in a breeze when there is a good ripple on the water.

ABOVE: A large brown trout caught fishing a wet fly on a floating line on the Clywedog Reservoir in Wales.

Claret. When constructing a team it is normal to put the slimmer, heavier patterns on the point and middle dropper with the bushier, palmered flies on the top dropper. These bushier flies have more water resistance and work well when dibbled in the surface.

Wet fly fishing from the bank is also effective on lakes, and the basic set-up and flies are similar to those used from a boat. The water is covered by the angler making a cast, retrieving the line then taking a pace. Headlands are usually good places to find fish especially if the wind is blowing across or into them, bringing food within casting distance of the bank. Lure fishing on stillwaters is basically a scaled-up version of modern wet fly fishing. The same floating and sinking lines are used, only they are heavier for casting and retrieving the larger lures.

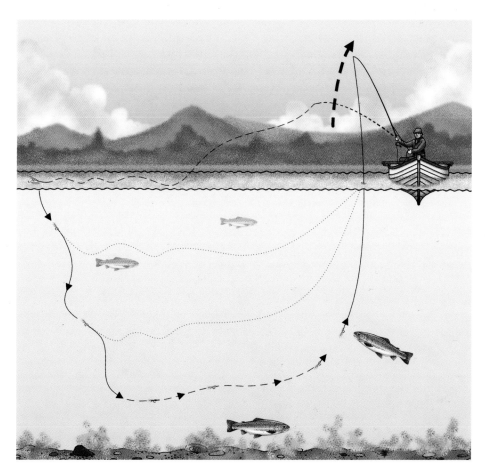

LEFT: The modern style of fishing a team of wet flies on a reservoir designed to find the level of the fish. The angler casts to (a) with a sinking line and then by counting allows the line to sink to various depths (b), (c), and (d), although this technique need not be confined just to three levels. When the flies reach (d) they are drawn up and allowed to hang vertically in the water for a few seconds as trout often follow the flies and take when they are nearing the surface.

Lure Fishing

In most forms of angling, lures refer to spinners, plugs or pirks, but in fly fishing it is the term used for large fly patterns usually tied on size 8 longshank hooks and above. Many lure patterns are very brightly coloured – orange, pink and white are particular favourites, though in contrast the combination of black and fluorescent green is a deadly one, especially during spring and the early summer months. Lure fishing for brown trout and rainbows is usually confined to stillwaters.

ABOVE: **The figure-of-eight retrieve.**

Lure Fishing on Stillwater

Some anglers regard lures merely as attractors or stimulators of the trout's aggression, but they can play an imitative role too. The most obvious example of this is as fry imitations, patterns designed to suggest coarse fish species such as roach and bream. Trout will often take quite large fish up to 3 in (7.5 cm) or more in length and for an imitation to be effective it must be a similar size to the prey.

Although lures can be fished on heavy wet fly tackle, their large size and air resistance means that they are better fished on specialized rods and lines. Lures may be fished on all densities of line, from floating down to the fastest of sinkers, including Hi-D and Di-7, plus lead core if the fish are in really deep water. Patterns such as floating fry, which imitate a small dying fish hanging in the surface, are best fished on a floater, but other patterns work well fished right down to the lake bottom. On average, though the most productive depth of water is 8–15 ft (2.44–4.57 m). From the bank 6–10 ft (1.83– 3.05 m) is the optimum depth, but in very hot or cold weather the trout can be much deeper, and some way of reaching this depth of water is needed. If a boat is not an option a reservoir's dam wall is often the place to find the deepest water accessible from the bank and can be the most productive area to fish, both early and late in the season.

From a boat a lure may be fished either at anchor, where the boat is used as a casting platform, or on the drift where it is allowed to follow the wind covering a large area in the search for fish. Drifting may be accomplished either side-on to the wind – similar to loch-style wet fly fishing – or pointing down the wind. Side-on drifting works extremely well when the fish want a slowly moved lure and allows the angler to control the depth at which it fishes easily. When fish are in the mood to follow right up to the boat it also makes "hanging" the lure possible. This can be a deadly method in which the lure is left to hang static for a number of seconds a few feet below the surface, where this change in pace often entices a following fish into taking.

Drifting with its point down the wind allows the boat to move more quickly, its direction being controlled either by a rudder or a drogue attached to the stern. This technique, often known as Northampton-style, allows two anglers to cast out either side of the boat, letting the line swing round in a large arc before being retrieved. This arc covers a vast area

BELOW LEFT: **A reservoir angler chooses another lure from a well-supplied fly box.**

BELOW: **Reservoir fishing from the bank. Long casting may be necessary.**

of water and, by using a fast-sinking line, a large part of the water column can be searched. By using lines of varying sink rates or by counting down before starting the retrieve the lure may be fished at different depths until takes are forthcoming.

As long-distance casting is often necessary from the bank, most lures are fished either on a weight-forward or shooting-head line. The shooting head, constructed from 10–12 yds (9.14–10.97 m) of fly line connected to a shooting line such as braided or plain nylon monofilament, is used where distance is required. In the right conditions this set-up is capable of being cast 40 yds (36.6 m) or more.

Tackle for lure fishing includes a rod 9½–10½ ft (2.9–3.2 m) long capable of casting an 8–10 weight line. Ordinary weight-forward lines may be wound on standard reels designed for 8–10 lines, but for shooting heads a large-diameter model keeps the turns of backing as open as possible and helps prevent tangling.

Retrieve rates should also be varied. In the early season when the water is still cold a slow, steady figure-of-eight retrieve is the most effective. Later in the year when the water has warmed up and the fish are more active a fast strip often works better.

An exception to this is when fishing the Booby, because even during warm weather this buoyant-eyed pattern is most effective when fished extremely slowly, on a fast-sinking line and a 3 ft (0.91 m) leader, along the lake bottom.

Whatever the type of lure, the key is to keep varying the retrieve rate until the effective one has been found. Because of the large size of the flies used, leader strength should be from 6–10 lb (2.72–4.54 kg) breaking strain. Lures may be fished singly or in teams of two or three on a 12–15 ft (3.66–4.57 m) leader with the second pattern on a dropper 4 ft (1.22 m) from the point.

Effective lure patterns include the Cat's Whisker in the original white and fluorescent green plus other colours, the Whiskey Fly, Black Leadhead and the Booby. When trout are taking fry the Deer Hair Fry, Zonker, Minkie and large, white patterns such as a single or tandem Appetiser will catch the most fish.

RIGHT CENTRE: A beautiful silver rainbow caught on a Booby.

RIGHT: Playing a trout on Lough Corrib, the famous trout lough in Ireland, on a fine still day. Conditions do not always have to be perfect for the angler to be successful.

ABOVE: Playing a big trout caught on a lure.

Flies

Fishing flies fall into two categories: those that are tied to imitate a natural item of the fish's diet and those flies, including nearly all salmon flies, that are intended as attractors, gaudy concoctions that have often caught more fishermen than fish. Fashions in flies change frequently. Twenty or thirty years ago trout flies were tied to mimic the natural insect as closely as possible and salmon flies were works of art with romantic names such as Lady Caroline and Green Highlander. Today patterns of trout flies have become far more standardized, one pattern being used as an imitation of a number of natural insects, while salmon flies are infinitely plainer, and generally more successful.

Wet Flies

Wet flies are designed to sink and often incorporate water-absorbent materials and swept-back wings and hackles to help achieve this. They vary in make up from simple spider patterns to more complicated tying such as the Silver Invicta which has a palmered body hackle and a wing. Although a number are tied to imitate specific insects, either aquatic or terrestrial, the majority are tied as attractors or simply to suggest something alive and edible.

Sooty Olive

This traditional wet fly is a great favourite on the big limestone loughs of Ireland. It imitates the emerging nymphs of the dark lake olives, *Cloeon simile,* which hatch out in prodigious numbers during May and June. It is worth trying on any stillwater where there are hatches of the natural fly.

Zulu

This striking pattern is another traditional stillwater fly and is most effective on either lake or reservoir. It is particularly deadly for wild brown trout and may be fished either on the point or the top dropper of a three fly cast. The Blue Zulu tied with a blue hackle is almost more popular. Use natural seal's fur for the body.

March Brown

The true March Brown, *Rithrogena germanica*, is a fly of freestone rivers. The imitation, with its hare's fur body and subtle shades of brown, is probably even more useful as a general "suggestive" pattern as it resembles different sedges and moths. It works well on either river or lake and used to be a popular salmon fly.

Claret Dabbler

Developed by Donald McClarn for fishing the loughs of Ireland the Dabbler is a great fly to fish as a top dropper fly, and often moves a number of fish even in a big wave. Dabblers are tied in a variety of colours including olive, yellow and fiery brown and are probably taken for sedges by the trout.

Kate MacLaren

The Kate MacLaren is a great fly when lake fishing for brown trout, sea trout and, in its larger sizes, it has taken salmon, too. It is generally fished as a top dropper fly and works especially well when "dibbled" through the tops of waves in rough conditions.

Peach Palmer

With its body of fluorescent peach wool, the Peach Palmer is a modern twist on a traditional wet fly profile. A superb rainbow trout pattern, it is at its best during sunny conditions on a reservoir fished fast on an intermediate or slow-sinking line.

Peter Ross

This is a traditional pattern and is equally effective on river and lake. With its silver and red body and speckled teal wing it resembles a small fish and has caught countless sea trout and wild brown trout. It is slightly less popular now than some years ago.

Gosling

This Irish fly pattern is an imitation of the mayfly, *Ephemera danica*, and is most effective during late May and early June. Although the natural mayfly is yellow the added brightness of a hot orange hackle only makes the Gosling even more deadly.

Doobry

Hailing from the Orkney Isles, the Doobry looks just like a traditional loch fly but was developed quite recently. The design is based on the Zulu with a palmered body and red tag. It is an excellent fly for the top dropper; the black and orange hackles make a great colour combination after rain when the waters of the shallow lochs in the Orkneys are stained with peat.

Oakham Orange

Developed for fishing on Rutland Water, the Oakham Orange is a superb summer fly when the rainbow trout are feeding on daphnia, the tiny plankton that inhabit the lakes and reservoirs of the Midlands. It works well at all depths and can be retrieved at a slow to medium-fast pace. Taff Price's Orange Nymph is another good fly to try when trout are feeding on daphnia.

Dunkeld

This garish fly is a scaled-down version of the fully dressed salmon fly. This version of the Dunkeld is used for trout and sea trout on stillwaters. It is a good general pattern and can be taken as a small fish or sedge pattern. It also works well when the trout are feeding on daphnia when it should be fished quite slowly. It may be tied with a palmered or throat hackle.

Palmered Coch

Based on a traditional imitation of the Coch-y-Bonddu beetle, the Palmered Coch is effective throughout the season especially for wild brown trout. It is at its best fished slowly on a floating line. Although the Coch-y-Bonddu works best during a fall of beetles in June, it will also take fish beneath the surface and is used as an imitation of a number of beetles.

Mallard and Claret

The subtle shades of the body and wing make the Mallard and Claret a great pattern when the sky is overcast. The Grouse and Claret, and Teal and Claret, are similar traditional loch flies that have stood the test of time. It is an effective pattern on both river and lake. It is a popular fly for sea trout at night, although it takes both brown and rainbow trout as well.

Black Pennell

Part of a small range of patterns, including the Claret Pennell. The Black Pennell makes a passable imitation of a midge pupa. It could be held to represent any number of black midges and beetles to be found in stillwaters and many anglers always include a Black Pennell on their cast. This version, with a thicker dubbed body, is an excellent pattern for both sea trout and salmon.

Bibio

An Irish pattern, created by Major Charles Roberts of the Burrishoole Fishery. The Bibio was tied to represent the heather beetle for sea trout fishing. It is now a well-established pattern for lake fishing, effective for brown and rainbow trout. It is a particularly good pattern in the warm weather of August when the natural fly falls on the water.

Kingfisher Butcher

One of a series of patterns including the Silver Butcher and the Bloody Butcher, with its bright-blue tail and orange hackle this is the most colourful of the tribe. It is a favourite fly on Loch Leven, the famous trout loch in Scotland, where Mary, Queen of Scots, was held prisoner. It is a good fly to try when fishing lakes with attractors and resembles a small fish.

Soldier Palmer Muddler

This fly is a hybrid of two classic patterns: the Soldier Palmer, a well-known traditional palmered loch or lake fly that imitated a sedge, and the Muddler Minnow with its deer-hair head, first tied in 1967 by Don Gapen. The combination makes a deadly lake fly for all species, and the Soldier Palmer Muddler is a highly suitable top dropper fly for when there is a good wave.

Teal, Blue and Silver

With its sparkling silver body and slim teal wing the Teal, Blue and Silver bears an uncanny resemblance to a small fish. Along with the Teal and Red, and Teal and Green, it has been a popular fly on Scottish lochs for 200 years. It is a good fly for both lake and river, especially for sea trout, in sizes 8 to 10. It is also effective when blue damselflies are on the water.

Claret Bumble

The original bumbles came from Derbyshire and date back to Charles Cotton of *Complete Angler* fame. The modern bumbles were designed by T C Kingsmill Moore for the Irish loughs, and the Golden Olive Bumble and Claret Bumble are the best known. They are effective both for brown trout and sea trout in a good wave. The original blue jay is better as the shoulder hackle.

Silver Invicta

This is the silver-bodied version of James Ogden's classic fly, the Invicta, which has a yellow wool or seal-fur body. The Silver Invicta is a successful lake and reservoir pattern working well throughout the summer. Like the parent fly it is a good imitation of a sedge, or hatching sedge but it is also one to try when trout are taking tiny "pin fry".

Nymphs and Bugs

Nymphs and bugs cover a large group of patterns designed either to give the impression of something alive and potentially edible to the fish or specifically to imitate an aquatic creature such as a shrimp. Others are tied to represent the various stages such as larva, pupa or nymph which make up the life cycles of aquatic insects including midges, damselflies and caddisflies. Many nymph and bug patterns are tied with weighted bodies to help them sink.

Cased Caddis

This heavily weighted pattern imitates a caddis larva complete with its case. It works best fished "dead drift" on rivers or inched slowly along the bottom of a lake. It is a great fly in the early part of the year when trout are low down in the water.

Griffiths' Damsel

Developed by Terry Griffiths, this is a good general representation of an olive damselfly nymph. These are readily taken when the flies are hatching. Fish it with a steady figure-of-eight retrieve on either a floating or intermediate line.

Distressed Damsel

This Charles Jardine pattern is an impressionistic imitation of an olive damselfly nymph. Its long tail of dyed marabou gives it a superb action in the water, and it can be deadly when fished with a steady figure-of-eight retrieve. Opinions differ as to whether trout take the colourful adult fly as well as the nymph, and dressings such as a sunken Camasunary Killer can be effective.

Woolly Worm

This simple bug-looking fly is a good suggestion of something alive and edible. It is best fished slowly along the lake bottom either on an intermediate line or a floating line and a long leader, and may be taken for a caddis larva, damselfly nymphs or leeches. It is a popular fly in the West Country, where it has the reputation for taking large fish. It can be tied in a variety of colours.

Fox Squirrel Nymph

Designed by American fly-tying legend Dave Whitlock, the Fox Squirrel Nymph is a good general pattern and may be taken for a damselfly nymph. Using the fur from a red fox squirrel it works well on either river or lake. In larger sizes it works best when heavily weighted.

Claret Emerger

Emerger patterns, which imitate an aquatic insect as it hatches out at the water's surface, have revolutionized stillwater trout fishing. This Jeremy Herrmann pattern should be fished very slowly just under the surface or allowed to float statically in the surface film.

Mobile Bloodworm

Bright-red chironomid larvae (bloodworms) usually spend their lives concealed in a silt tube. However, when disturbed, they swim with a manic lashing of their body. The soft marabou tail of the Mobile Bloodworm attempts to imitate this movement. They are a staple item in the diet of stillwater trout.

Flash-back Pheasant Tail

The Pheasant Tail Nymph invented by Frank Sawyer is an effective fly in its own right, but add a modern touch of sparkle using pearl plastic tinsel, and you have a deadly variation. The Flash-back Pheasant Tail is effective on both rivers and lakes when the nymphs are hatching.

Ascending Midge Pupa

This imitation of a chironomid midge pupa works well when trout are feeding on the natural, and can be taken at any depth from mid-water to the surface. To imitate the natural pupa it should be fished extremely slowly on the point of a long leader together with a floating line.

Lead Bug

Constructed almost entirely of lead wire, this little fly sinks extremely quickly and is ideal for stalking trout in clear stillwaters. Fished on a floating line and long leader, it should be cast at individual fish and retrieved very slowly. Watch out for takes on the drop.

Stick Fly

Tied to imitate a cased caddis larva, the Stick Fly should be made with an underbody of lead wire to help it sink quickly. A highly competent fly for early to mid season, it works best fished on a floating line and long leader, retrieved slowly along the bottom.

Czech Nymph

This style of nymph has had a huge impact on river fishing for both trout and grayling. It is heavily weighted, sinks very quickly and is fished on a short line in the "rolled nymph" method (see page 220). This is a great fly when the fish are feeding on the bottom and is particularly effective in the autumn. A number of dressings have been evolved to suit this style of fishing. All of them incorporate weight to help them sink.

Longshank Pheasant Tail

The reservoir version of Sawyer's classic Pheasant Tail Nymph, this pattern is tied big on a longshank 8 or 10 hook. The thorax colour may be varied from yellow to orange, green or black. A pearl thoraxed version is particularly good when trout are feeding on pin fry, although the original is a representation of the lake olive nymph. Arthur Cove's version, tied as a buzzer without tails, is a useful stand-by on many lakes.

Prince Nymph

With its peacock herl body this general nymph pattern works well on small lakes and reservoirs. Tied with a weighted underbody it may be fished singly for individual fish or as the point fly of a team of three when it has a chance to sink down in the water.

Shipman's Buzzer

Developed by reservoir expert Dave Shipman, this pattern represents a chironomid midge pupa about to transform into the adult. Greased-up and fished right in the surface film it may be left static, to be intercepted by a cruising trout or retrieved steadily.

Walker's Mayfly Nymph

The late Dick Walker developed this pattern as an imitation of the large pale nymphs of the mayfly, *Ephemera danica*. It works well not only on rivers, where the naturals are to be found, but also on lakes where it is probably taken as a damselfly nymph or hatching sedge. Tied with a heavy lead underbody it is an excellent fly for targeting trout in small clear stillwaters where the individual fish can be spotted.

Montana

Originally an American imitation of a large, dark stonefly nymph, the Montana is now more often used as a general nymph pattern to imitate a number of insects on stillwaters, and is probably taken for a dragonfly nymph. When tied weighted, it is best fished slowly on a floating or intermediate line but it can also work well when retrieved fast with the leader degreased to avoid line wake in calm conditions.

Gold-head Hare's Ear

The Hare's Ear is one of the best traditional representations of the hatching olive nymph. It is normally tied with just a few strands of the hare's fur picked out as the hackle or pale starling wings. Recently fly tiers have added a gold bead at the head of the original dressing, and this glint of gold has been a real attracting magnet for trout and grayling both in rivers and stillwaters.

Classic FM

In this olive version the Classic FM makes a good imitation of a damselfly nymph. Fished on a floating or intermediate line with a slow figure-of-eight retrieve, the marabou tail works superbly and stimulates the movement of the original as it rises to the surface. Even if damselfly nymphs are not hatching this fly gives the impression of something edible and has been used with success on many waters.

Skinny Buzzer

Reservoir trout eat midge pupa in vast numbers. This pattern imitates the profile of the pupa extremely well and, being slim, cuts through the water quickly to go down to the trout's feeding level. As with all buzzer patterns, fish this ultra-slow on a floating line and long leader.

Shrimp

This pattern imitates the small freshwater shrimp, *Gammarus pulex*, which is to be found in large numbers on both rivers and lakes. It is tied with a heavy lead underbody to help it sink quickly and easily and is best fished quite slowly along the bottom.

Dry Flies

Dry flies are intended to float on or in the water's surface. Many, particularly the modern ones, are tied with buoyant or water-repellent materials such as polypropylene, Antron or deer hair to prevent them sinking. A large proportion of dry fly patterns, especially those designed for use on rivers are imitative rather than impressionistic, tied to represent specific aquatic insects such as mayflies, caddisflies and various species of olives.

CDC Caddis

The soft, downy texture of Cul de Canard is perfect for tying the wings of a variety of insect imitations. Here the CDC provides the roof-wing profile of an effective adult caddis pattern that is fished on the surface. Most caddis patterns work best early in the year and are fished on or near the bottom.

Klinkhammer Special

Hans Van Klinken came up with this original-looking and highly effective pattern. Tied parachute-style, where only the hackle and wings float, it was designed to imitate an emerging caddis. It is deadly on rivers for both trout and, particularly, grayling when naturals are hatching.

Shadow Mayfly

This bushy dry fly bears little resemblance to a real mayfly. However, the combination of palmered grizzle hackles for the body and red game hackle points for the wings produces a simple pattern that is extremely effective during a mayfly hatch, when it is often taken rather than more realistic patterns.

Yellow Humpy

A buoyant fly, the Humpy is designed for fishing in turbulent water for it is a superlative floater and is easily visible in rough water. When it is cast upstream it should be allowed to bounce back on the riffle when the trout come at it extremely quickly. A great pattern for freestone trout.

Adams

An American design and probably one of the most popular dry-fly pattern used by anglers today. The Adams is superb on all types of water, especially on rivers. It is a great general pattern and particularly effective during a hatch of medium olive duns.

Bob's Bits

This simple stillwater dry fly is the brainchild of Bob Worts. With its teased-out seal fur body, the Bob's Bits sits low, right in the surface film and is deadly during a midge hatch when it imitates the hatching insect trying to break through the surface film. It is tied in many colours: red, orange, olive and black.

Sparkle Dun

This is a variation on the Comparadun, a very effective pattern for difficult trout when they are taking duns off the surface. The Sparkle Dun not only has a tail of Antron but also a polypropylene wing to help it to float, and there is no hackle, to ensure the overall profile is as lifelike as possible.

Parachute Grey Duster

The Grey Duster is an immensely popular dry fly on both rain-fed rivers and chalk streams. This is the parachute version where the hackle is wound on a small post on top of the hook. This allows it to fish right in the surface film, emerger-style, imitating the emerging nymph.

Foam Beetle

A simple little pattern tied on a size 16 to 18 hook, the Foam Beetle sits low in the water. It is a great pattern to try on finicky trout either on river or lake. This is definitely one to try when fish are taking small terrestrials in a flat calm, on those evenings when one fish will be a triumph. Fish it very slowly indeed.

Pheasant Tail

A simple, impressionistic fly, the Pheasant Tail is an effective pattern on all types of river. Its overall profile makes it one to try when trout are taking duns, but when it is sparsely dressed and fished right in the surface film. It is an excellent imitation of the olive spinner for the evening rise.

Mayfly Spinner

With its outstretched wings this imitates the spinner of the female mayfly as it lies trapped in the surface film when it has laid its eggs. At this stage it is taken eagerly by trout that, at times, appear as if they have been waiting all day. There are a number of patterns, and it is a good idea to have several available in the fly box. Change the fly if the first pattern does not work.

Blue Damselfly

Although this fly will spend most of its time in the fly box, when trout are taking adult blue damselflies in the summer it is one of the best patterns to try and certainly the most successful. High summer, when the naturals are patrolling the lake margins, is the time to give this a cast and it should be fished to imitate the quick flight of the natural insect.

Red Tag

This is a classic grayling pattern, some 150 years old, and it is particularly effective on rain-fed rivers. It is a great fly for the winter months, when the river is low and clear after the first frosts, and may be tied and fished either dry or wet.

Hare's Ear

Any fly pattern incorporating mottled brown hare's fur is going to be effective. This tying is no exception, working extremely well both as a general pattern and during a hatch of olive duns, particularly in the first months of the year.

CDC Dun

Cul de Canard is a wonderful material for all kinds of dry fly wings, but it is probably most effective for imitations of olive duns. Here it is used for the CDC Dun, a superb pattern for both lake and river. The clipped thorax hackle keeps the pattern as sparse and as realistic as possible, and it is one of the first patterns to try.

Elk-hair Caddis

Al Troth's Elk-hair Caddis is a simple robust imitation of an adult caddis or sedge fly and is effective when used for both. With its buoyant elk-hair wing and palmered body it floats well and may be drifted with the current when fished on a river or twitched to mimic the movement of the natural, fishing in the sedge hatch on lakes.

Claret Hopper

Although called a Hopper this fly has has nothing to do with grasshoppers. Instead it is an extremely popular stillwater dry fly that is at its most effective during a hatch of large brown midges. It is tied in a range of colours including claret, orange, olive and black. There are over 400 species of midges $\frac{1}{8}-\frac{3}{4}$ in (3–20 mm) long, so the problems of imitation for the angler is obvious. When the trout are feeding on midges it can pay to try a number of different patterns if the first is not accepted.

Royal Wulff

The Wulff series of flies, with their V-shaped hair wings, was invented by the late Lee Wulff, one of the most celebrated American anglers. The Grey Wulff and White Wulff are often used on chalk streams when mayflies are hatching. It is a style of tying incorporated into many patterns, and this – the Royal Wulff – is a version of the classic Royal Coachman and makes a superb general river pattern. The Coachman is said to have been invented by a Royal coachman over 150 years ago and represents a white-winged sedge.

Greenwell's Glory

Originally tied by Canon Greenwell for fishing the River Tweed, on the Scottish–English border, the Greenwell's Glory is still a fine imitation of small- to medium-sized olive duns. It is fished upstream and allowed to drift drag-free with the current. The Greenwell's Nymph is also effective.

Black Gnat

Tied to imitate a specific insect, the *Bibio johannis*, the Black Gnat can be used to suggest a wide variety of small black creatures. It may be tied in a range of hook sizes from 12 down to 22. The smaller sizes are particularly deadly when trout are feeding on tiny black midges or smut (black insects).

Daddy-longlegs (Crane Fly)

This is an imitation of the daddy-longlegs or crane fly, a terrestrial insect most often seen during the cool damp months of autumn. The Daddy has a reputation for enticing the bigger fish and is often used when dapping on lakes and lochs. Otherwise it is recommended that it is fished on a floating line and allowed to lie stationary on the water. There are a number of patterns: the most popular uses knotted pheasant tail fibres to represent the trailing legs of the natural insect.

G&H Sedge

If you need a really buoyant sedge pattern, then this is the one to choose. The G&H Sedge uses spun and clipped deer hair to form the roof-wing profile of the sedge and works equally well on rivers and lakes. In larger sizes it even works for salmon when they can be induced to take a dry fly. Sedges emerge at dusk and on a river can provide the most exciting half hour of the evening rise before darkness falls. They are equally prolific on stillwaters and lochs.

Hairwings

Normally tied on large hooks hairwings include many of the lures and flies used for salmon fishing on rivers and trout fishing on reservoirs. Normally used as a wing, hair is a tough material and works well on patterns designed to fish where the current is strong and would flatten softer feathers. Although some artificial hair is now used, bucktail, stoat and squirrel's tail are the most popular and are available in a wide range of natural and dyed colours.

Goldie

This was developed by Bob Church for big Rutland Water brown trout. The Goldie can be tied either on a single longshank hook or two, in tandem, if a really large lure is need. It is best fished on a fast-sinking line from either a boat or the bank. It is reminiscent of the popular black-and-yellow tubes used for salmon in spring and autumn.

Whiskey Fly

This hot-orange lure is a real killer during the summer months when trout are taking daphnia – a tiny animal plankton. Fish feeding on daphnia will often go mad for orange flies, and the Whiskey Fly fits the bill. It works best when fished quite fast on an intermediate or normal sinking line. Let the line sink before starting the retrieve.

Sweeney Todd

A Dick Walker pattern, the Sweeney Todd is a good early season fly on reservoirs and small stillwaters. The fluorescent magenta aiming point, at the throat, was intended to stimulate the trout into taking the fly near the head, thereby reducing the number of missed takes. It has been one of the most successful lures for many years.

Mickey Finn

This colourful hairwing uses fine mylar tubing to create a sparkling body. It is a popular reservoir pattern for the summer and originated in America. It is at its most effective in the summer months when the water temperatures are high and it is taken by rainbow trout. Like most lures it should be stripped fast through the water.

Woolhead Sculpin

This is a modern imitation of a sculpin or bullhead, a small bottom-dwelling fish most commonly found on rivers. It has a habit of fooling the larger, more predatory trout. The fly is very similar to the Muddler minnow, another imitation of the sculpin.

Blackie

Originally a reservoir lure, the Blackie is also a highly effective fly when sea trout are lying deep. It works best after midnight, fished on a fast-sinking line to get right down to the fish. It is tied either on two hooks in tandem or with a flying treble.

Deer-hair Fry

Trout will often specifically target small coarse fish as they float dying near the surface. This buoyant design, which uses spin and clipped-deer hair for its body, imitates this phenomenon superbly and should be fished almost static on a floating line.

Zonker

The Zonker uses a strip of rabbit fur still on the skin as a highly mobile wing and tail. In its natural grey form it is a fantastic fly to use when trout are feeding on fry. Tied in other colours, such as white, black and pink, it is a fine general lure pattern.

Streamers

For mobility and action there is little to beat feather as a winging material, and streamers and feather-winged patterns are extremely effective on many types of water. Although cock hackles were once the most commonly used material, they have been almost entirely superseded by marabou. This soft, ultra-mobile feather is now used to produce the wings and tails on a large number of patterns for reservoirs and small stillwaters, because combined with a weighted body or head, it provides the fly with an almost irresistible action.

Leprechaun

Devised by Peter Wood the name, not surprisingly, comes from its bright-green colour. An effective pattern during bright summer days when there is a lot of algae in the water.

Muddler Minnow

This is the tying of Don Gapen's original Muddler, created to imitate a small fish. The technique of spinning and clipping a deer-hair head is now used in a range of lures and imitative patterns.

Dawson's Olive

Although basically a lure, the subtle combination of varying shades of olive gives this fly a very natural appearance, and it may be taken as a damselfly nymph or other creature. Fished slowly on a floating or intermediate line it works on all types of stillwater. Watch out for takes on the drop.

Junglecock Viva

The is a scaled-down version of the original Viva, named by its creator after the Vauxhall car. Tied on a double hook and with Junglecock eyes, it is a great point fly for sunk line fishing out of the front of a drifting boat. The action of the boat works the fly and takes fish in all conditions and a variety of waters.

Idiot-proof Nymph

Not a nymph at all, the IPN uses a soft marabou tail plus a weighted Fritz body to deadly effect. It is tied in a wide range of colours, including black, olive, orange and pink, and can be fished on either a sinking line or as a floater with a long leader. Either way it is a lure worth trying for stocked rainbows.

Black Leadhead

A superb pattern on all types of lake and reservoir the Leadhead, with its mobile tail and weighted head with its painted fish eye, produces a ducking/diving action when it is retrieved that trout cannot resist. It can be tied in a range of colours with black, white and orange among the most successful.

Mrs Simpson

This New Zealand pattern uses layers of pheasant body feathers for the sides. It is best fished slow and deep on lakes. It is a passable imitation of a dragonfly nymph and may be taken as such by trout.

Mylar Fry

A good imitation of a fish, the Mylar Fry works well when trout are feeding on tiny roach fry and sticklebacks. It is best to fish this lure slowly on a floating or intermediate line.

Concrete Bowl

This pattern was tied specifically for fishing on large man-made reservoirs, a number of which are simply concrete bowls. Black and green is a deadly colour combination for lake trout, and this lure is no exception.

Medicine Fly

This Hugh Falkus pattern was designed specifically for sea trout on rivers. It is tied light and slim for when the river is running low and clear during the summer. The body may be either fine silver tinsel or just silver paint.

Yellow Booby

Love it or hate it, the Booby is a devastatingly effective pattern when the trout are feeding hard on the bottom. It should be fished on a fast-sinking line with a short leader of about 3 ft (0.91 m) and retrieved very slowly. Boobies are available in a variety of colours all of which can work well including yellow, white, black and green.

Orange Cat's Whisker

The original version of the Cat's Whisker has a white marabou wing and tail plus a fluorescent green body. The profile is now tied in a range of colours and the version illustrated here is the all-orange one. Usually fished on a sinking line the Cat's Whisker is often taken on the drop as the lure descends through the water.

Ace of Spades

This twist on the Black Chenille lure uses a matuka wing capped with bronze mallard to produce a dense profile. The Ace of Spades works well early on in the season, and should be fished slowly along the bottom using a sinking line. It was invented by David Collyer and is effective in dark water.

Black Rubber Legs

The kicking action of the rubber legs is one that stillwater trout find difficult to resist. This pattern is deadly on all types of water. The pattern should be weighted and fished with a twitchy retrieve to accentuate the leg movement on either a floating or intermediate line. This stimulates the fish to take.

Appetizer

Bob Church tied this reservoir pattern back in the early 1970s specifically to imitate roach fry. It proves effective to this day, tied on either a single longshank hook or two in tandem if the trout are taking larger fry. Fish it on a sinking line from either bank or boat, although a slow sinker is best in shallow water.

Haslam

This is a traditional feather-winged pattern that is extremely popular in Wales for both salmon and sea trout. It is normally tied on size 6 and 8 salmon hooks and may be fished on a floating, intermediate or sink-tip line depending on the water conditions and temperature. It works best in the summer.

Minkie

A superb fry imitation, this Dave Barker pattern uses a mobile strip of grey mink fur as its wing. It is most effective when fished slowly, on a sinking line, around weed beds and other areas which hold shoals of coarse fish fry that the trout chase after in summer when the fry have just hatched.

Hairwing Salmon Flies

Old-fashioned salmon flies were tied with many feathers as their wings. They remain objects of great beauty. Nowadays a salmon may be caught on one occasionally, but they are generally just used as a last resort. Modern salmon flies even those based on old patterns, are simpler in design and easier to tie. Many use hairwings as this gives them more life in the water. All should be tied in a variety of different sizes to cope with different water levels.

Hairy Mary

A popular salmon fly similar in colour to the feather-winged Blue Charm. It may be tied on single and double hooks as well as tubes and Waddington shanks. It is a fly that is most often used in the summer when the salmon are taking smaller flies in duller colours fished on the surface with a floating or sink-tip line. It is a good fly for grilse.

Garry Dog

This bright fly is tied either on doubles and trebles or, in larger sizes, on tubes and Waddingtons. On some rivers it is used all the year round but it is generally a fly for the autumn or spring when yellow-and-black and plain yellow colours seem to work best. It is also successful in the evenings when fish will take a fly a size or two larger.

Executioner

This handsome-looking fly, with its flash of red and silver and junglecock cheeks, hails from the River Kent in Cumbria. It was originally tied as a sea-trout fly but it has proved an excellent fly for salmon as well. It works well in the summer and is usually tied on smaller-sized hooks. Fish the Executioner on a floating or sink-tip line.

Stoat's Tail

This all-black fly with just a hint of sparkle is probably the most popular salmon fly of all. It may be tied on single, double and treble hooks, and if a particularly large fly is required, on either a tube or Waddington shank. In its smaller sizes it is also very good for sea trout. A Silver Stoat's Tail with a silver body and black wing is also good.

Willie Gunn

This is a superb fly for either spring or autumn salmon fishing and may be tied on either tubes or Waddington shanks. The most effective sizes are from $1^{1}/_{2}$–$3^{1}/_{2}$ in (4–7.5 cm) long. It is made up of yellow, orange and black hair tied on top of each other, often on a copper tube when a sinking fly is required.

Mini Tube

When the water is clear and low, salmon often respond best to tiny patterns. A Mini Tube should be fished on a floating line and is a fly for summer fishing. It may be tied in a range of colours, although blue and black are the most useful and it can be very small indeed. It may be difficult to get small enough trebles.

Ally's Shrimp

This versatile pattern was developed by Alastair Gowans, one of the best salmon anglers, and is one of the most popular salmon flies in use today. It works right through the season in various water conditions. Its long-tail style is said to imitate the natural shrimp of the sea and has now been copied in a number of other patterns.

Munro Killer

An extremely popular salmon pattern, the Munro Killer has an ultra-long wing of mixed bucktail to give it plenty of fish-attracting movement. It is a highly effective fly throughout the season and particularly in the autumn when the leaves are turning colour and salmon seem to prefer orange-coloured flies.

Baits

There are a number of ways of catching game fish other than with a fly. When water conditions dictate, the use of artificial baits such as spinners and plugs or even natural ones, including worms and prawns is perfectly legitimate, depending on the regulations that apply to the water you are fishing. A number of salmon rivers may be "fly only" or fly only during certain months of the year, and similar restrictions may apply to trout lakes and reservoirs. Although frowned upon by some, bait fishing for trout and salmon does work. In ordinary water conditions it can sometimes be very effective. However, when the river is high and coloured and fish are not responding to a spinner, let alone a fly, it can be the only method of catching fish.

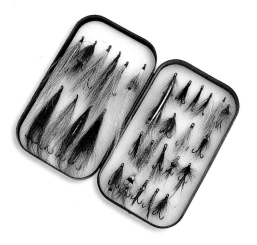

ABOVE: Large salmon flies have much in common with minnows.

Natural Baits

If you are fishing on a river that permits the use of baits either all the year round or when certain water conditions prevail, then there are two main natural baits to try.

Worms

Although various baits can be used, including maggots and more natural ones such as caddis grubs, the two most popular are worms and shrimps.

Worms are effective for trout, grayling, sea trout and salmon. For trout and grayling a single worm or a bunch of small worms, such as brandlings or gilt tails, is perfect. However, for sea trout and salmon the use of two or more large lobworms is usually more effective. They can either be fished with a spinning rod with the aid of a bubble float, if allowed, or cast gently upstream with a fly rod and allowed to rumble down the river bed.

Shrimps and Prawns

These are the saltwater variety of baits preserved and dyed various colours such as red and purple. Shrimps can be extremely deadly, and on a number of rivers their use is prohibited. They also have the reputation of causing a strong reaction in the salmon. Either they take it forcefully or are unsettled by them and bolt out of their lie, so many anglers frown upon the use of shrimps. However, in big heavy water the much larger prawn can sometimes prove the only method of catching a fish so, where allowed, it is a worthwhile method in difficult conditions. Both are prepared in similar ways. First they are straightened and a sharp-eyed needle is inserted through from head to tail. Then the hook is attached and the whole thing bound with elasticated thread to keep it together.

Artificial Baits

Artificial baits for salmon and trout consist of a large variety of spinners and spoons. Some are more popular than others.

Rubber Tails

Rubber Tails, or Flying Condoms as they are less politely known, have taken salmon spinning by storm and in their various colour combinations are now the most widely used

LEFT: A successful angler nets a small salmon caught on a spinner.

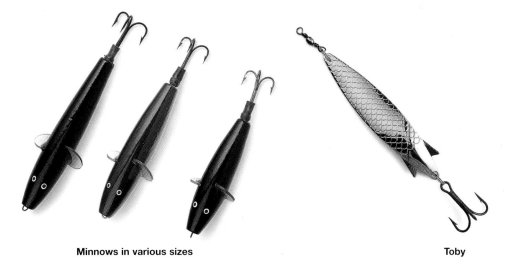

Minnows in various sizes

Toby **Rapala sinking lure**

spinners in the UK. They come in a variety of types with either a plain or beaten metal blade or with a small revolving minnow at the front. Whichever type, they all have one thing in common: a soft vibrating rubber tail which salmon find irresistible. Rubber tails come in a choice of weights from 7–20 g and in a variety of colours, such as red and gold, red and silver, black and gold, and yellow and gold.

Toby
Once the most commonly used spinner for salmon, it is manufactured by a Swedish tackle company and produced in a range of sizes, weights and colours. Copper, silver and gold are particular favourites although a zebra pattern and the multi-coloured Toby Flash are also very effective. For heavier water there is also the Toby Salmo range, a broader, heavier spinner at 30 g, as well as a super-lightweight version available only in blue and silver at 8 g for use in summer conditions.

Devon Minnows
With the profile of a small fish, the aptly named Devon Minnow is a great favourite among salmon anglers. Devons come in a wide range of sizes and colour combinations. Black and gold, blue and silver, and brown and gold are particularly effective, the darker colour always being on the minnow's back. They are available in sizes ranging from 2–3¹/₂ in (5–8.9 cm) and in weights from 8 to 20 g.

The closely related quill minnow, being much lighter than the Devon, is most effective in clearer, slower-moving water. Here the lightness of the minnow works superbly even in the reduced flow rate and is ideal for

catching trout and sea trout when the river is low.

Rapalas
Various models of Rapala are becoming increasingly popular for salmon fishing. Their darting action makes them much more lifelike in the water than the traditional Devon Minnow although they are considerably more expensive. The most popular models in the range are the Original Floating and the Countdown in blue, gold and brown although the newer Husky Jerk with its superb action and built-in rattle has become extremely well-liked.

ABOVE: A fine fresh spring salmon taken on a Devon minnow.

In larger sizes the diving action of the Countdown, the Shad Rap and the Husky Jerk makes them extremely effective when trolling on big lakes for salmon and brown trout, particularly in the early months of the year.

Mepps
For spinning in clear, shallow water there is little to beat the Mepps. In its smaller sizes it works well for trout and in larger sizes for trout and salmon. With their weighted body and revolving metal blade Mepps come in sizes ranging from the tiny size 0, which can only be cast without extra weight on the lightest of rods, up to size 5 which is more than adequate for salmon.

Weights
Not all spinners and baits are heavy enough to be cast without extra weight. Split shot or drilled bullets are commonly used for bait fishing; it is easier to fish them in the rocky, tackle-hungry pockets where fish hold. For spinning more specialized weights, the Hillman Anti-Kink Lead and the Wye Lead are often used. Remember though to use lead-free weights.

Swivels
When using any type of spinner it is important always to use at least one swivel to prevent the line from twisting. While ordinary barrel swivels are perfectly adequate for salmon fishing or when trolling for large brown trout, ball-bearing swivels are far better. Although more expensive the advantages of ball-bearing swivels over the standard type are that they are not only extremely strong, but they are able to revolve even under the pressure exerted by a big fish.

Fly Tying

Tying threads

While all the flies you will ever need can be purchased, there is something extremely satisfying about catching a fish on a fly that you tied yourself. On a practical level the ability to tie flies enables old favourites or new patterns to be created with a specific hatch or set of conditions in mind. This not only brings the angler one step closer to understanding how fish behave, but it also contributes to the evolution of fly tying.

Tools

For many experienced fly fishers the ability to tie flies and to fish go hand in hand. And even for the novice, with a little practice and a bit of practical advice, the ability to tie simple but effective flies is only a short time away. The first step is to select the right equipment.

Vice

The most important tool of all is the vice. This fits on the tying bench and grips the hook firmly between metal jaws, allowing the tyer enough room to apply all the various materials. When choosing a vice it is vital to ensure that the jaws really can grip both large and small hooks securely. Rather than choosing the cheapest vice, go for something reasonably priced instead. Preferably it will be a lever-operated model that allows the tyer to exert the right amount of pressure by depressing a cammed lever to the rear of the vice.

Fly-tying vice

Scissors

At least one pair of sharp fine-pointed scissors is needed both to prepare materials and to trim off any excess or wayward fibres. It is better to have two pairs, however. The first can be used for cutting tinsel or other tough materials, such as wool or quill, while the other can be kept for trimming hackle fibres etc.

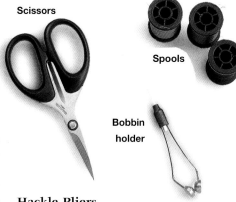

Scissors

Spools

Bobbin holder

Hackle Pliers

This small sprung-wire tool grips hackles and other fine materials between its jaws, allowing them to be wound easily without being damaged by the fingers. Make sure that the hackle pliers you choose have rubber-covered jaws to prevent them cutting delicate hackles.

Bobbin Holder

The bobbin holder helps the tyer apply the tying thread, while keeping waste to a minimum. It also provides additional weight which allows the thread to be left hanging while still retaining enough tension. This prevents the materials already applied from unravelling. Always choose a spigot bobbin holder, preferably one with a ceramic tube. The ceramic is extremely hard and smooth, and never damages the thread, unlike the old-fashioned metal ones.

Whip-finish Tool

With its sprung metal arms, the whip-finish tool is a great help to those who find the task of whip finishing – completing a fly – difficult merely using the fingers.

Dubbing Needle

This simple little tool is used for teasing out dubbing materials, freeing any trapped fibres, hairs or feathers and applying varnish.

Materials

Next come the materials, all the furs, feathers and other bits and pieces which actually make up the various fly patterns. Not surprisingly the selection is vast. However, when beginning fly tying it is better to choose just a few of the most popular materials and get used to using those before becoming more adventurous.

Tying Thread

This is the fine, strong thread which holds the fly together. Originally natural silk was used, but today man-made rot-proof products, such as nylon, are the most popular. Tying thread comes in a wide range of colours, although black, brown and olive are the most used.

Tinsels

Tinsel

Tinsel provides a fly with sparkle and comes either in a flat strip, as a round thread or as a wire. Once metal, modern tinsels are either coated or

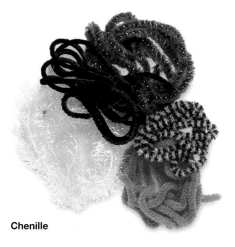

Chenille

made from plastic to prevent tarnishing. Silver and gold are the traditional colours but pearl lurex is very popular in modern patterns.

Wool

With its coarse texture wool is ideal for winding or for teasing out and dubbing on to create a chunky body. It can also be used for tails. Wool comes in a wide range of colours, both plain and fluorescent.

Chenille

French for "caterpillar", chenille certainly has a worm-like appearance and is usually wound along the hook to create a dense succulent body. It comes in a wide range of colours and diameters, and can be used for lures right down to small nymphs.

Cock Hackles

These feathers come from the neck of a domestic chicken and are used for tails, wings and, most commonly, for the hackles of wet and dry flies. Cock hackles come in a wide range of natural and dyed colours.

Marabou

This downy feather comes from a domestic turkey and is available in plain white plus a whole range of dyed colours, including fluorescents; however white, black and olive are the most popular. The texture of the marabou gives it a superb pulsing action and it is used widely in tying reservoir lures and tadpoles.

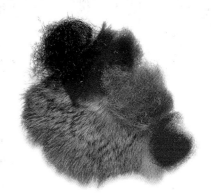

Hare's fur and dubbing materials

Dubbing

Many furs, such as hare, rabbit and seal, are used for dubbing. They come in a vast range of natural, dyed and blended colours and may be used for the bodies of wet flies, dry flies and nymphs. Man-made products, such as Antron and polypropylene, are also widely used, particularly for dry flies.

Floss

Floss is available in a wide range of colours and is normally wound along a hook to a create slim, tapered body. Silk was the original material but rayon, which winds flat and smooth, is very popular today. Recently, stretchable products have become more widely used.

Feather Fibre

Many types of feather, such as pheasant tail, ostrich and goose quills, are used either plain or dyed to create soft, natural-looking bodies in a variety of nymph and dry-fly patterns. Sections of wing quills from either the mallard duck or starling are also used for the wings of wet and dry flies.

Hooks

Fly hooks come in a range of sizes and types from the minute size 24 for tying the smallest of dry flies right up to 3 in (7.5 cm) Waddingtons used for salmon. Between these two extremes the most popular hook patterns for trout and grayling flies include round bend wet fly in sizes 10–16, lightweight dry fly in sizes 12–18 and longshank hooks in sizes 4–12. For salmon the hooks are larger, from size 4–10, and these can be either singles, doubles or trebles. If a really big fly is needed a tube or a Waddington shank combined with a treble hook allows flies up to 3 in (7.5 cm) or more to be created.

Olive cock cape

Coral marabou feathers and Superfloss

Marabou feathers

Natural and dyed cock capes and saddle patches

57

Getting Started

Once you have obtained a good range of tools and materials it is time to put them to use. Before getting to grips with all the intricacies of tying flies it is a good idea to learn a few simple techniques such as how to fix the hook in the vice and how to start off the tying thread. Also, what is often forgotten at this stage but is extremely important, is how to finish a fly off securely. There is little point going to all the effort of tying a fly if, after you have added all the materials, you cannot stop the thread unravelling and the fly falling to pieces.

Fixing the Hook in the Vice

The first step when tying a fly is to fix the hook in the vice. The object is to secure the hook so that it doesn't move as you wind the thread but there is enough of it showing to allow easy application of the materials.

Most fly-tying vices have jaws where the gap can be altered by turning a knurled wheel just in front of the lever. This allows various sizes of hooks to be gripped securely. To fix the hook, insert the bend of the hook in the jaws and depress the lever firmly with the free hand. If after depressing the lever fully the hook is still loose, turn the wheel so that the gap decreases slightly. Adjust the gap a little at a time until it is small enough so that the jaws grip the hook firmly when the lever is fully depressed.

Once the gap is adjusted correctly it is time to position the hook. There are various ways of doing this but the best is to have just the bend of the hook gripped by the jaws with all of the shank and the point of the hook showing. Some fly tyers advise having the point of the hook masked by the jaws to prevent it snagging the tying thread and breaking it while you are tying. This can happen and it is a nuisance when it does, but masking can damage the hook which is more serious, and it is better to have as much of the hook showing as possible as this makes it easier to tie in all the materials you need.

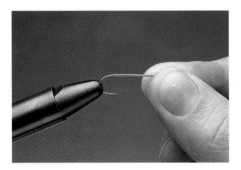

1 Offer the hook up to the jaws and see if it fits, so that the hook is held firmly in the vice.

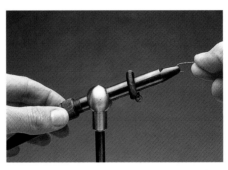

2 If the gap is incorrect adjust the jaws with the knurled wheel until it is slightly greater than the thickness of the hook.

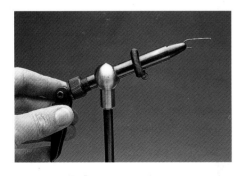

3 Depress the lever fully to grip the hook firmly. If necessary you can loosen the jaws slightly to adjust the hook's position.

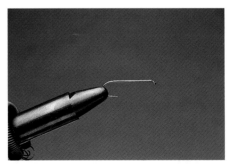

4 Ensure that the shank of the hook is horizontal and only the bend is masked. You can then apply the materials more easily.

The Whip Finish

With the tying thread in place you are now almost ready to tie a fly. But first you must learn how to finish off. It may sound back-to-front but without learning how to finish off a fly securely all your efforts will be wasted – your creation will simply fall to bits when being cast.

The best and most secure way of accomplishing this is with a whip finish. Here the thread is wound over itself to form a loop which is drawn tight, thus holding the loose end of the thread secure. Either fingers or a special whip-finish tool can be used to create a whip finish. Here a tool has been used since it is the most commonly employed method, especially for novices.

The whip finish is normally made once all the materials have been added and a small head formed. However for ease of illustration the sequence uses a bare hook and floss rather than normal tying thread.

Starting the Tying Thread

With the hook fixed firmly in the vice and in the correct position it is time to apply the tying thread. Tying thread is used to hold all the other materials in place so it is the first thing to be fixed to the hook. Tying thread is normally run on at the hook's eye and then taken down the shank where the first materials are caught in and secured at the tail of the fly.

The method is to loop the tying thread over the shank and, while holding the loose end taut, wind the other end of the thread over it and the hook shank. This puts the thread under friction and secures the loose end in place. It is important to prevent the thread slipping off as you wind it in. It sounds quite easy but it can be a little tricky for the beginner so this is a technique worth practising. To help illustrate the correct procedure thicker floss which is more visible, rather than tying thread, has been used to illustrate this sequence.

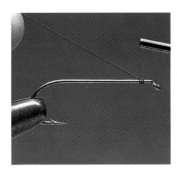

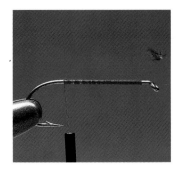

1 Loop the tying thread over the shank holding the loose end of the thread above with the thumb and forefinger of your left hand and the bobbin end, which will be wound round the hook, below in your right.

2 Holding the thread taut using a bobbin holder, begin to wind the thread down the shank so that it covers the loose end. Five or six turns will be enough to prevent the thread from unravelling from the hook.

3 Cut away the excess loose end with sharp scissors before continuing to wind the thread down to the bend of the hook. Some tyers apply a dab of clear varnish to the hook to help to hold the fly together.

4 Wind the thread down the shank to a position opposite the hook point. Ensure that the thread turns are closely butted and flat so they form an even base for the materials that are to follow them.

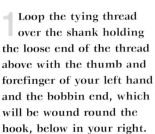

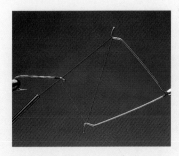
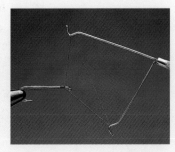
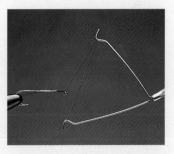

1 Assuming the fly has been completed, take hold of the tying thread and loop it over both hooks of the whip-finishing tool so that it makes a triangle.

2 Flip the tool over. This will form one turn of the whip finish and make one turn of the loop over the loose end of the tying thread on the hook.

3 Repeat the process four or five times adding an extra turn of the loop over the loose end every time. This will create a firm whip finish.

4 When enough turns have been completed flip the thread off the top hook and, keeping tension with the lower hook, pull the loose end of thread. This draws the loop closed and ensures a tight even finish to the head of the fly.

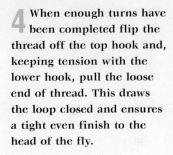
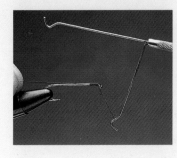
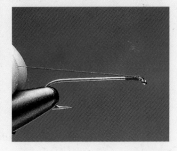

5 Finally, remove the lower hook and pull the thread tight. The head of the fly can now be varnished to prevent the thread wearing. Some of the following fly patterns have coloured heads.

Tying Sequences

Nymph: Pheasant Tail Nymph

The Pheasant Tail Nymph is a traditional nymph pattern invented by Frank Sawyer on the Hampshire Avon and is effective on both rivers and lakes. It can be tied in a variety of sizes to suggest a wide range of small invertebrates. This version differs from the original, having a hare's-fur thorax instead of plain pheasant tail fibres.

This pattern demonstrates how to tie a feather fibre body, build a simple thorax common to all nymphs and rib the body of a fly.

Hook: **size 16 wet fly–size 8 longshank**
Tying Thread: **brown**
Tail: **cock pheasant tail fibres**
Rib: **copper wire**
Body: **cock pheasant tail fibres**
Thorax cover: **cock pheasant tail fibres**
Thorax: **hare's fur over copper wire**

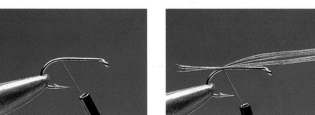

1 Fix the hook in the vice, catch in the tying thread and run the tying thread down the hook shank to a point opposite the barb.

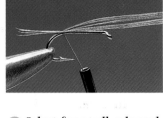

2 Select four well-coloured cock pheasant tail fibres and catch them in so that the tips project past the bend to form the tail.

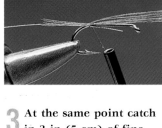

3 At the same point catch in 2 in (5 cm) of fine copper wire. This will form the rib. Secure this with the tying thread.

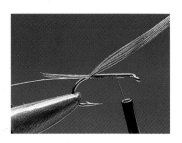

4 Wind the tying thread back up the shank towards the eye in neat touching turns. Stop two-thirds of the way along.

5 Take hold of the pheasant tail fibres and now wind them over the shank in close turns so that there are no gaps. Secure the ends with the thread.

6 Wind the copper wire over the body in four or five open, evenly spaced turns. These should be wound in the opposite spiral to the pheasant tail.

7 Secure the end of the rib before cutting away the excess feather. Then, catch in another slip of pheasant tail fibres just where the body ends.

8 Wind the end of the copper wire over the remaining shank, building a distinct lump. This both forms the thorax and adds extra weight to the fly.

9 Wax the tying thread, then take a pinch of hare's fur and dub it with a finger-and-thumb twist on to the tying thread. You only need a little.

10 Wind the dubbed fur over the copper wire to form the thorax of the nymph. Allow plenty of hairs to stick out. These mimic a real nymph's legs.

11 With the thread just behind the eye, draw the pheasant tail fibres over the back of the thorax and secure them in place with the thread.

12 Remove the excess feather and build up a small head. Complete the fly with a whip finish and secure the head with a drop of varnish.

Hackled Dry Fly: Red Tag

A simple but deadly pattern, the Red Tag is a great
favourite with many anglers fishing for trout and grayling.
It is the traditional fly to use for grayling in the winter. It
can be fished either wet or dry, but the latter method is
most commonly used.

This tying sequence illustrates how to tie in a wool tail,
a peacock herl body, which is used in a number of dressings,
and a collar hackle common to the majority of dry flies.

Hook: **size 12–18 light wire dry fly**
Tying Thread: **brown**
Tail: **red wool**
Body: **peacock herl**
Hackle: **natural red game cock**

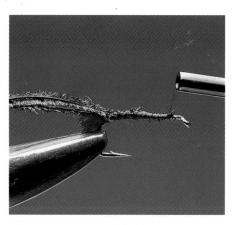

1 Fix the hook in the vice and run
the tying thread on down to the
bend in touching turns, creating a
solid base for the body. Cut away the
excess tying thread.

2 At the bend, catch in a tuft of red
wool to form the tag. Position the
wool on the top of the hook and allow
the waste end of the wool to lie along
the hook shank.

3 Select three or four strands of
peacock herl and catch them in at
the base of the tail. Secure the waste
ends along the shank, winding the
tying thread back up the hook.

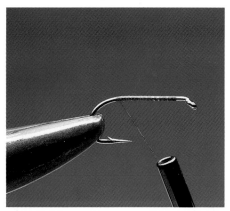

4 Twist the peacock herls together
and wind the rope over the shank
to form the body. The herl on the
peacock fibre will stand out to form
the body. Tie them in at the head.

5 Trim off the excess herl and select
a natural red game cock hackle
with fibres slightly longer than the
hook gape. (A natural red game hackle
is actually brown.)

6 Remove any broken or downy
fibres from the hackle base and
catch it in just behind the eye, leaving
a short section of bare stem. Make
certain it is secured properly.

7 Take hold of the hackle tip with a
pair of hackle pliers and wind on
three or four full turns to form the
collar hackle at the head of the fly.
This is the way to put on all hackles
used when tying dry flies.

8 Secure the hackle point with the
tying thread before removing the
excess. Build a small neat head and
complete the fly with a whip finish
and a dab of clear varnish. Trim the
red tag at the tail if necessary.

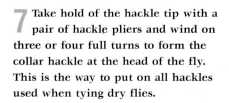

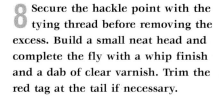

Winged Wet Fly: Invicta

The Invicta is a classic winged wet fly and is most effective during the summer months on lakes and rivers. Tied large it makes a good sea-trout pattern for loch fishing but it is at its best when used for brown and rainbow trout on reservoirs and lakes. It is especially successful during a hatch of sedge flies as it is an excellent imitation of hatching sedge pupa.

This pattern illustrates how to tie a dubbed body, a palmered hackle and a wet fly wing.

Hook: **size 14–8 medium-weight wet fly**
Tying Thread: **brown**
Tail: **golden pheasant topping**
Rib: **fine oval gold tinsel**
Body: **yellow seal fur or substitute**
Body Hackle: **red game cock hackle**
Throat Hackle: **blue jay**
Wing: **hen pheasant centre tail**

1 After fixing the hook in the vice run the tying thread to a point opposite the barb. There, catch in a golden pheasant crest feather plus 2 in (5 cm) of fine gold tinsel.

2 Take a pinch of yellow seal's fur or a man-made substitute such as Antron. Dub it on to the tying thread with a simple finger-and-thumb twist. This will form the body of the fly.

3 Add the fur thinly to create a fine but fluffy rope. That done, wind the rope along the shank towards the eye. Ensure that there are no gaps and that the effect is even.

4 Once the body has been wound select a natural red game cock hackle with fibres slightly longer than the gape of the hook. Judge this by bending the hackle against the hook as shown.

5 Prepare the hackle by stripping off any down or broken fibres from the base to leave a short section of bare hackle stem. Catch this hackle in just behind the eye of the hook holding it securely in place.

6 Take hold of the hackle tip with the pliers. Wind the hackle towards the tail in open, even turns. Ensure that no fibres are trapped. This technique is called palmering and is used on many traditional patterns.

7 Once this body hackle has been wound to the base of the tail take hold of the fine gold tinsel and make one turn over the hackle tip holding it in place. Make sure the tinsel is flat and without kinks.

8 Continue winding the gold tinsel up over both the body and hackle towards the eye. The turns should be evenly spaced and are intended to lock the hackle turns in place. It is easier to do than it appears.

9 Secure the rib at the eye with thread turns before removing the excess tinsel and feather. Take a pinch of blue jay and catch it in under the body as a throat hackle.

10 Take a slip of golden pheasant centre tail three times the width of the intended wing. Fold one edge to the centre of the slip then fold it in half to form the wing.

11 Offer the wing up to the hook and secure it in position with thread wraps. The first turns of thread should pull directly downwards to prevent the wing from twisting.

12 Remove the excess feather before building a neat head and casting off the thread with a whip finish. Complete with a drop of clear varnish to the head.

Acknowledgements

The publishers wish to thank the following individuals and suppliers for their help and the loan of equipment for photography:

Dave Ellyatt
Drennan International Limited
Bocardo Court
Temple Road
Oxford OX4 2EX
Tel: (01865) 748989

Mike Ashpole
Ashpoles of Islington
Green Lanes
London N16
Tel: (020) 7226 6575

Brian Frattel
Farlows
5 Pall Mall
London SW1Y 5NP
Tel: (020) 7839 2423

Martin Ford
27 Willesden Avenue
Walton
Peterborough PE4 6EA
(01733) 322497

Andrea Barnett
Hinders of Swindon
Ermin Street
Stratton
St. Margaret
Swindon SN3 4NH
Tel: (01793) 333900

Lyn Rees
Shimano (UK) Ltd.
St. John's Court
Upper Forest Way
Enterprise Park
Llansamlet
Swansea SA6 8QR
Tel: (01792) 791571

Fishing suppliers:
Lawrence Short
Trace Ace
PO Box 236
Chatham
Kent ME4 6LF
(01634) 848839

Tony Caton
Gemini Tackle Co.
Gemini Works
Mill Lane
Caistor
Lincolnshire LN7 6UA
(01472) 852966

Relum
Carlton Park Industrial Estate
Kelfale
Saxmundham
IP17 2NL
(01728) 603271

PICTURE CREDITS
The publishers would like to thank the following people for their kind permission to reproduce pictures in this book:

Inside: Peter Gathercole – pp 1; 2; 4-5; 6-7; 8; 9; 10 b; 11; 12 cr & bl; 13; 14; 15; 16 bc; 17; 18 bl; 19 br; 27 br; 28; 29; 30; 31; 32; 33; 34; 35; 36; 37; 38; 39; 40; 41; 42 bl; 43 tr; 44; 45; 56 bl; 57 bc.
Tony Miles – p 19 tr.
Bruce Vaughan – p 42 tr.
John Wilson – p 19 bl & cr.

key: r = right, l = left, t = top, tl = top left, tr = top right, tc = top centre; c = centre; b = bottom, bl = bottom left, br = bottom right, bc = bottom centre.

Index